DEE BROWN
MY ILLINI YEARS

The News-Gazette

SP
SPORTS
PUBLISHING
L.L.C.

SportsPublishingLLC.com

The News-Gazette.

Editor and publisher: John Foreman
Executive editor: John Beck
Managing editor: Dan Corkery
Sports editor: Jim Rossow
Photo editor: Darrell Hoemann

Publishers: Peter L. Bannon and Joseph J. Bannon Sr.
Senior managing editor: Susan M. Moyer
Developmental editor: Doug Hoepker
Art director: K. Jeffrey Higgerson
Cover design: Dustin Hubbart
Interior layout: Kathryn R. Holleman
Imaging: Dustin Hubbart, Heidi Norsen, and Kenneth J. O'Brien
Photo editor: Erin Linden-Levy

© 2006 by *The News-Gazette*

ISBN: 1-59670-171-4

Front cover photo: John Dixon/*The News-Gazette*
Back cover photo: Jonathan Daniel/Getty Images

Printed in the United States of America

Sports Publishing L.L.C.
804 North Neil Street
Champaign, IL 61820
Phone: 1-877-424-2665
Fax: 217-363-2073
SportsPublishingLLC.com

CONTENTS

FOREWORD

BY BRETT DAWSON
THE NEWS-GAZETTE
MARCH 29, 2006

I knew Dee Brown was a player the first time I saw him. But it took me a little while longer to realize he was something more.

I'll never forget the steamy July day when I first saw Brown on a basketball court. It was at Bill Self's Chicago satellite camp at the Moody Bible Institute. Brown was a featherweight guard back then, heading into his senior year at Proviso East High School, and the trademark braids were in their infancy as a close-cropped afro. But the speed was apparent. The deep shooting range, too.

Though I didn't know it until a few days later, Brown committed to Illinois that very afternoon—one of my first days on the job at *The News-Gazette*. A few days later, I saw Brown again, this time as a visitor to his home in Maywood, Illinois. A photographer and I came to town to profile a kid whom Self—and later Bruce Weber—would come to call "the poster child of Illinois basketball." It was that afternoon when I realized that Brown wasn't a mere basketball player. He was a personality unlike any other I'd met.

The plan that day was for the photographer to get a few shots of Dee and his mother, Cathy, and for me to have a sit-down interview with the kid they called "The One-Man Fast Break." That turned into a walk down to the park where Brown sometimes played basketball, and a viewing of his high school football and basketball highlight films. By the time we left, night had fallen and I'd stuffed a notebook and tape recorder with quotes and anecdotes—something I would become accustomed to in the years following when interviewing Brown.

Covering Dee Brown was unlike covering any athlete I've encountered. One day during his freshman season, Brown declined to speak with reporters. The next day he apologized, face to face, with a handshake. I could provide countless other examples of how valuable an asset he was to those of us whose job it is to cover the team.

Brown has told me on many occasions that his freshman year seems like only yesterday. But to me, it seems like a long time ago. In fact, though I covered a full season before he arrived on campus, it's hard sometimes for me to imagine Illinois basketball without Dee Brown. There will be other stars in the orange and blue, certainly, but there might never be another with the same combination of charisma and hoops acumen. Brown's mind moves as quickly as his feet, his quips as dazzling as his assists. He has been even more reliable in a press conference than on the court, which is really saying something considering he was always good for at least one "Did you see that?" play each night.

That summer evening at Brown's Maywood home, I was taken in by that highlight video of his, by a buzzer-beating three-pointer and an impressive quarterback scramble. But pictures are only half the story with Dee Brown. You need his words, too. We've done our best to collect some of his most memorable here. Here's hoping you enjoy reading them as much as we enjoyed writing them down.

Dee Brown acknowledges the crowd during a speech at 2005's Midnight Madness at the Assembly Hall. *Robert K. O'Daniell/The News-Gazette*

INTRODUCTION

BY DEE BROWN

During my time at the University of Illinois, I got excited for every game I played. But sometimes I think my family was even more excited than I was. When I was growing up, we never had the opportunity to go to big-time basketball games, or to travel outside of our area. So when I came to Illinois, suddenly my family had a chance to do something they had never done before.

Every game, I could look into the stands and see my family. My mom was there, or my brothers. They had the opportunity to travel all over the country to watch me play. It seemed like they went to every state in the process. And they got so excited watching me play, that I couldn't help but get a little more excited myself. That's the kind of thing I'll think about when I remember my time at Illinois.

Of course, I'll also remember the fans. I think our fans have made me stronger, and that's why I want to thank them from the heart. The best thing about Illinois fans is that they're so supportive. At any school, you have your fair-weather fans. But our fans are amazingly supportive. To play in front of them at the Assembly Hall—to hear them clapping, to hear people calling my name—is one of the best feelings I've ever had. Everywhere we go, they're going to come see us, no matter where we are. That's the support that Illinois fans have for our basketball program. You can't deny them, and I'll always appreciate them for that.

People always talk about my legacy at Illinois. I've heard people say that there are recruits who consider coming to Illinois now because of me—that I helped raise the profile of the program. But I don't think about that. I really don't. The way I look at it, when I got here, Illinois was already on the rise. It was on the way to being something special. While I was here, things came together and it happened. We had a Final Four run. We won the Big Ten title outright twice. That's what I'll remember when I think about my time at Illinois. I won't think about my impact. I'll just think about how much fun I had. I'll think about all the great guys I played with and all the love and support I received from the community.

People talk about what I've meant to Illinois, but Illinois made me what I am. That's why I'll bleed orange and blue forever.

Dee Brown gestures to the bench before the start of Illinois' 2005 Final Four matchup against Louisville at the Edward Jones Dome in St. Louis.
Ronald Martinez/Getty Images

FRESHMAN YEAR

AP/WWP

THE PIED PIPER

Dee Brown Commits to Illinois

By Brett Dawson, *The News-Gazette*
JUNE 24, 2001

Dee Brown's head is huge. Not his actual head, mind you, which is merely head-sized. And not his figurative head, either, for though the Proviso East point guard is confident, he's not particularly boastful.

No, the gigantic cranium in question is a black-and-white duplication of Brown's head, photocopied and pasted on the body of Jamal Tinsley, the former Iowa State point guard. There are literally dozens of these Brown heads, scattered all over the 2000-01 Iowa State media guide, some well-proportioned to the photo of Tinsley's body on which they've been placed, others blown wildly out of scale, caricature-style.

"They did it on every picture of him, pretty much," Brown says, leafing through the pages of the guide, one of thousands of mailings he's received in the past three years. "He wears my number, 11, so they just put my picture over his head. It's pretty creative, really."

It takes a little something special to stand out in the sea of mail that comes every day to the apartment Brown shares with his mother, Cathy. Some days there are as many as 200 pieces, and though some will end up thrown away, many of them are stuffed into a large green hamper, most of them unopened.

They'll keep coming, too, though Brown might read them even less now. Last week, he took the first step in ending the recruiting process, giving an oral commitment to Illinois. Brown's mailbox

Dee Brown brings the ball up the court during the 2002 McDonald's high school All-American game at Madison Square Garden in New York City.
Al Bello/Getty Images

still will be stuffed, though, and his phone likely will keep ringing at all hours.

"I'm glad just to have it out of the way, but I think coaches will keep calling me," says Brown, one of the top high school point guards in the Class of 2002. "I hope they do, just to see how interested they are in me. I mean, I'm good with Illinois. But if another coach calls, I'm not going to hang up on him."

Which should come as no surprise to anyone who knows anything about 16-year-old Daniel "Dee" Brown. He rarely passes up an opportunity to talk.

TALK THE TALK

It's always been that way for Brown. Though he was quiet on the court when he first took up the game, he's never lacked for words off it. Cathy Brown laughed when she referred to her son as "Mr. Popularity," and John Maestranzi, who's coached Brown in summer ball for four years, said even as an eighth-grader, Brown, "was always a talker."

"When we go to these AAU events in the summer, it doesn't matter where we go, Indiana, Oklahoma, wherever, he knows everybody," Maestranzi said. "He just likes to get out and meet people, and he's always making friends with all those guys when they're hanging out between games or whatever."

In three years as a starter at Proviso East, he's already broken the school's career assists record, and last season he averaged 19 points and dished out eight assists a game. Those numbers, and the speed Brown uses to rack them up, earned him the nickname "The One-Man Fastbreak" and made him an attractive commodity to a host of schools in the Big Ten and beyond. The names pursuing him — Illinois, Michigan State, Iowa State — were huge. Brown, you might have heard, is not.

SIZE MATTERS

For all the talking he's willing to do, the topic many seem to favor is the height thing.

"The big knock on him is his height," said Rob Harrington of Prep Stars, a North Carolina-based recruiting service. "That's the thing that a lot of people harp on about him."

Brown stands 5-foot-11, though he's quick to point out, with a laugh, that he's "maybe 5-11 1/2 with the 'fro."

"Watch this," Brown says, pointing to the small TV screen near the foot of his bed. "See this kid right here? That's Mark Pancratz, from Schaumburg. He's guarding me right here. He's about 6-3, something like that. He's a great defender. Great defender."

The clip sees Pancratz, a fellow *News-Gazette* All-State first-teamer, trying desperately to keep Brown in front of him. Brown dribbles a step or two on the wing, then pulls up and drains a deep three-pointer.

"Look, I just raised up on him," Brown says, defiant. "That's a bigger guy trying to guard me, and I'm getting my shot off over him easy. That just shows you height doesn't mean that much. It's all how you play. How much heart you have.

"I play hard, and I've got heart."

FORWARD THINKING

It was during his sophomore season that Cathy Brown began to think Dee might be headed to the big time. And though she didn't want to overexert her influence, she let it be known that the closer to home Dee chose to go, the better. That played no small part in the ultimate decision to pass on Michigan State and Michigan and commit to Illinois. When Cathy took a liking to the UI program and campus, about a three-hour drive from Chicago, Dee's mind was all but made.

Dee Brown and his mother, Cathy, sit among a pile of letters Dee received from college recruiters and coaches. Jesse Evans/The News-Gazette

But he might not have selected Illinois were it not for the momentum the program picked up last year. Brown's game is a melding of the hardwood and the playground, but his heart is all Chicago city kid, and kids from the city despise nothing so much as losing.

"Oh, he hates it," Cathy Brown said. "We played Monopoly one year at Christmas, and his older brothers bought up everything. Boardwalk and everything.

"He didn't even have any money to pay the rent, so he had to quit. He was so mad. I had to tell everybody just to let him keep playing because he got so upset."

Brown wants to win. He wants to win at Illinois. And not surprisingly, he's not afraid to say so.

"Don't let anybody tell you different: Winning is everything," Brown said. "I like to talk, yeah, but nobody listens to it if you don't win."

BROWN COMES UP BIG

Freshman Guard Worthy of Honors

By Bob Asmussen, *The News-Gazette*
MARCH 2, 2003

No need to wait for the final week of the season. Mail in the ballot today and where it reads Big Ten Freshman of the Year, write "Dee Brown." With a thick marker.

Michigan's Daniel Horton has the higher season average and scored more points in their matchup Saturday. Doesn't matter. Brown's team won. And he hit the biggest shot.

Hey, Bill Self, did you think Brown was the best freshman on the court Saturday?

"I think he's the best freshman on the floor most nights," Self said.

That's a big "Yes."

The Illinois coach is the one who put the ball in Brown's hands with less than 90 seconds left and said, "Take the big shot." There's a reason the guy from Oklahoma has won 200 games at the age of

40. With the Wolverines holding a team meeting around Illini star Brian Cook, Brown nailed a 15-footer to give his team the lead. For good.

"I had to make a play," Brown said. "I can go 0 for 11, and I'm going to shoot it. That's just me. That's always been my thing. If my team needs me to step up and make it, hopefully I can step up and make it."

His teammates had no doubt he would come through. They have seen the confident point guard improve each day. During the team's four-game winning streak, Brown is averaging 16.8 points.

"Dee's definitely a clutch player," Illinois guard Sean Harrington said. "He showed that."

Illinois freshmen Deron Williams (left) and Dee Brown celebrate in the final seconds of the Illini's 82-79 win against Michigan on March 1, 2003.
AP/WWP

"Dee's not a freshman anymore," Illinois forward Roger Powell Jr. said. "We trust Dee shooting that shot. That's money."

Brown wasn't done helping. With 34 seconds left, he fired a pass to an open James Augustine in the lane for the basket that put Illinois up three.

"All week, we've been practicing that," Brown said. "I found him. That's my job."

Moments later, he tipped the ball away from Michigan and just missed a steal. He still had three, adding to his recent binge.

LONG GONE

Two weeks ago, on a snowy night in West Lafayette, Ind., Brown ended a nasty five-game stretch with a 2-for-10 shooting performance against Purdue. He made 28 percent of his shots and Illinois went 3-2, losing at Michigan State and Purdue. Clearly, he's gotten over it.

"It never bothered me," Brown said. "I was worrying about the team. There weren't any Dee Brown issues. It's about Illinois basketball. I didn't play well in a couple games, but I rebounded. And I'm starting to play well when it counts."

That would be the opposite of what Horton is doing. When the Wolverines desperately needed the Texan, he blew a tire. Wednesday in a blowout loss at Wisconsin, he missed 10 of 11 shots. Saturday against Illinois, he missed 13 of 17. Michigan's hopes for a Big Ten title clanged away with each Horton brick.

Give Brown a good chunk of the credit for Horton's rough day. Brown pestered the taller guard.

"He didn't get in rhythm," Brown said. "I did a decent job on him. He'll rebound and do a better job."

Brown admitted to being extra fired up to play against Horton. Not for the awards, but for the challenge of it. The two got to know each other in the summer while playing on the USA Basketball Junior World Championship team in Venezuela.

"I came out and tried to play hard against him," Brown said. "Daniel Horton did a pretty good job of running his team, he just didn't shoot the ball well tonight.

"Everybody was looking forward to the matchup. What's so good about him is he likes to compete. I'm more happy for my team performance than for my performance."

NO BIGGIE

Like all good leaders, Brown puts his team ahead of individual awards. Ask him if he was the best freshman on the court Saturday, and he quickly points to Michigan's Horton and Lester Abram, who had all 16 of his points in the first half.

"That Lester Abram cat is real good," Brown said. "He did an incredible job."

That Brown cat is real good, too. And when his team needs him the most.

"I definitely would take Dee over any point guard in the league," Harrington said.

Horton still is among the Big Ten's top 10 scorers and will get plenty of votes for the freshman award. But his conference title hopes ended when No. 11 stuck the jumper with 1:24 left.

Brown went home with the critical road win.

"Both teams played so hard," Brown said. "It's one of the greatest feelings in the world right now."

Take two more and Brown will celebrate a conference title.

"It's coming down to just getting the ring," Brown said. "I was emotional. This is a big win."

Dee Brown drives to the hoop against Michigan in the Illini's 82-79 win against the Wolverines in 2003. *AP/WWP*

FOLLOW THE LEADER

Personality, Talent Make Brown an Irresistible Illini

By Brett Dawson, *The News-Gazette*
JANUARY 5, 2003

The buzz started when Dee Brown hit Chalmers Street, built to a roar when he reached Daniel (no, it wasn't named after him) and didn't stop from there. By the time the Illinois freshman got to Wright and Green, he was the recipient of a standing ovation. At the epicenter of the Illinois campus. On a school day. This is the effect that Daniel "Dee" Brown, 18 years old and on top of his world, can have on people.

On a cool, clear day in December, Brown crossed campus to pose for the photo that accompanies this story, and he all but stopped traffic. The Orange Krush members set to pose with him chanted his name. Drivers craned their necks to get a look. Passers-by wondered what all the fuss was. The whole scene — the buzz that preceded him, the splash his arrival caused —

mirrored Brown's brief but eventful Illinois career to date, a wild 11-game ride that shows no signs of slowing down.

"I didn't ask for any of this," Brown said last week, after his image appeared in *Sports Illustrated* and after ESPN named him one of the nation's top freshman basketball players. "The whole thing is a surprise to me just like it is to everybody else. I just wanted to come in here and play basketball. All this recognition and everything? I had no idea."

But then, maybe it shouldn't be such a surprise. This is a guy, after all, whom Illini coach Bill Self said he envisioned from the start as "the poster child for Illinois basketball." This is a player who dazzles defenders (and crowds) with his

Dee Brown celebrates during Illinois' 70-40 defeat of Michigan State on Feb. 18, 2003 at the Assembly Hall. *Mark Cowan/Icon SMI*

speed, who energizes teammates with his very presence, who sends tape recorders into overdrive with his nonstop chatter.

"He's the future of our program," Self said. "By the time Dee is a junior, (the coaching staff) may not need to show up for practice. Dee might just be down there running things on his own."

Watching the impact Brown has had in the first half of his freshman year, it doesn't sound like such a stretch. Brown is scoring (14.1 points a game), he's setting up teammates (4.6 assists a night) and he's filling it up from downtown (39 percent from three-point range). And Self couldn't care less.

You want the real measure of Brown's impact? Watch a practice some Wednesday afternoon, when Illinois' battling the midweek blues, and Brown's energy gets his teammates going. Or talk to Brian Randle, the Illinois signee from Peoria Notre Dame who said Brown "played a huge role" in his decision to sign with the Illini. Or go walk the aisles at Dick's Sporting Goods in Champaign, where headbands are harder to come by than Tiger Woods bobblehead dolls.

ONE IN A MILLION

People are drawn to Brown, and it isn't hard to see why. He talks like a snowball rolling downhill and plays basketball like he's running late for a train. He's all reckless abandon, no restraint. He is at once a dream player for a fan, a coach and a TV camera crew.

How special? Tom Izzo said Michigan State has had two such players in the past 25 years, a couple of guys named Magic Johnson and Mateen Cleaves.

"When he steps in a room, everybody gets happier," said Illinois senior Brian Cook, a leader by example who's deferred some of the more vocal aspects of team leadership to Brown. "And when he's down, we can feel it."

HE LEADS, THEY FOLLOW

When the Illini play video games, Self said, it's Brown who gets everyone's competitive juices flowing with his trash-talking style. In study hall, Self said, it's Brown who turns grades into a competition, telling teammates who lose focus, "Go ahead and make a bad grade, then. I know I'm not going to."

"I don't think he gives you any choice but to follow him," Self said.

His influence even stretches off the Illinois campus and into high schools across the country. Charlie Villanueva, a top-five national prospect at Blair Academy in Blairstown, N.J., listed Brown, the host for his official visit to Illinois, as a primary reason he committed to the Illini. Same goes for Randle, who always liked Illinois but found the school even more appealing after Brown committed to the Illini and started making a recruiting pitch. It was just a few weeks after Brown committed to the Illini when he and Randle crossed paths at a high school summer tournament in Chicago.

"He was so friendly, and not just to me or to other (Illinois) recruits, but to everybody," Randle said. "It made Illinois that much more intriguing because you figure he's a guy that's going to impact the whole program, so if he's this much fun, a lot of the other guys probably will be, too."

BELIEVE THE HYPE

Cook said he's rarely played with anyone who makes the game more fun than Brown does, whether it's during a pressure-packed game against Missouri or a pick-up contest in the summer.

"I'm a people person, always have been," Brown said. "Some days I might be a little out of it,

Dee Brown poses in front of the Orange Krush student cheering section on campus. Members of the Krush sport the headband that Dee has helped to popularize among Illini fans.
Robert K. O'Daniell/The News-Gazette

not talking. But 23 days out of the month, I'm talking nonstop. That's my thing, just meeting people and talking. Before I die, I want to meet everybody."

That outgoing attitude has made Brown a go-to guy in postgame interviews, and it has brought him more than his fair share of attention early in his Illinois career. Self hasn't tried to curtail that publicity boom — Brown has been allowed to do as many interviews as he wants — but the coach does have his concerns about Brown getting too much too soon. But the freshman said there's no danger of the hype going to his cornrowed head.

"All I want to do is play basketball; that's all I've ever wanted," Brown said. "The recognition, that just comes with the territory sometimes. The more you get as a player, the more you want. So I just have to focus on improving my game. You can't be worrying about all the outside stuff. It's fun, but it doesn't mean anything."

OFF TO A GREAT START

Dee Brown's Freshman Year Recap

By *The News-Gazette*
MARCH 27, 2006

For more than a year before he arrived on campus, Dee Brown had Illinois fans as excited as they had ever been about a basketball recruit. The McDonald's All-American and *News-Gazette* All-State Player of the Year didn't disappoint, leading the Illini to a 25-7 record and a Big Ten tournament title. Averaging 12.0 points with a team-high 159 assists, Brown was a second-team All-Big Ten pick and a member of the Big Ten's All-Freshman team.

Paired in the backcourt with fellow freshman Deron Williams, Brown started a team-high 31 games.

"Right from the beginning, they've played beyond their years," then-Illinois coach Bill Self said of Williams and Brown. "I thought these guys could be good, and they haven't disappointed me."

Illinois won at least 25 games in each of Brown's four seasons, with his first campaign getting off to an 8-0 start. Brown never lost to Missouri, starting his streak with an 85-70 win in 2002 in which he had 21 points, seven assists and five rebounds despite a bruised shoulder.

"I would say that was an exceptional game," Brown said. "A typical game for me wouldn't be 21 points and five rebounds, four offensive. I'm supposed to be getting back on 'D.'"

There was no shortage of fun in Brown's first Braggin' Rights outing, one in a string of games that had him earning recognition as one of the nation's best freshmen.

Dee Brown pounds his chest in celebration after being fouled on a drive to the hoop against Western Kentucky in the first round of the 2003 NCAA tournament. *John Dixon/The News-Gazette*

"It's a great experience to go through with the crowd and the atmosphere," Brown said. "It's a learning experience, and I've got a lot to learn. I mean, I'm good, but I'm not that good."

Brown would go on to average 11.2 points in Big Ten games, second on the team only to future NBA first-round pick Brian Cook. He enjoyed several breakout Big Ten games, dishing out 11 assists against Penn State, scoring 18 points against Northwestern and scoring 16 in a rout of Indiana. But his regular-season highlight occurred against the coach who recruited him so aggressively, Michigan State's Tom Izzo. In a 70-40 Illini win at an all-orange Assembly Hall, Brown electrified the crowd with 24 points, five assists and five steals.

"People have to understand, I'm still a freshman even though I don't play like it sometimes," Brown said. "I've got a lot to learn as far as just being consistent and doing it every night."

DEE ON HIS FRESHMAN YEAR

What stands out to me about my freshman year is coming in with Deron Williams and James Augustine. We came in not really understanding our roles, unaware of how to play at the college level or how to play with a great senior leader like Brian Cook, who helped make us into the players we were. It was nerve-racking at times. It was my first time away from home, and everything was overwhelming. I remember spending a lot of time with Deron in the gym, just trying to get better, and hoping to figure out where we fit in at this level of basketball. My freshman year seems like yesterday to me, like Deron and I just moved into the dorms. And at that time, the older guys were telling me, "You're going to be a senior tomorrow." They told me the time was going to fly by, but I didn't really believe them. Now I know.

we can take with us to the (NCAA) tournament."

Brown backed up his talk by helping Illinois win its first Big Ten tournament title less than two weeks later, the point guard averaging seven assists in three wins. He was no less stellar in his

"People have to understand, I'm still a freshman even though I don't play like it sometimes."

–Dee Brown

The Illini contended for a Big Ten title until the final week. However, Wisconsin ended their hopes with a 60-59 win, as Devin Harris sank a last-second free throw after being fouled by Brown.

"I think we found out that we have a lot of courage and a lot of heart," said Brown, who scored 20 points. "We found some toughness that

NCAA tournament debut, with 16 points, eight assists and seven rebounds in a 65-60 win against Western Kentucky.

"If Illinois wins, absolutely he's the guy that drives the buggy," Self said. "He can be one of those guys. I thought he was just awesome. I thought this was one of his better moments."

DEE BROWN'S 2002-03 STATISTICS

OPPONENT	SCORE	FG-FGA	3FG-3FGA	FT-FTA	PTS	AST	REB	STL
Lehigh	W, 90-56	5-8	2-5	2-4	14	4	6	2
Ark.-Pine Bluff	W, 96-43	5-10	4-7	0-0	14	2	4	1
W. Illinois	W, 85-56	3-7	1-4	0-0	7	10	5	3
N. Carolina	W, 92-65	6-16	0-4	0-0	12	6	3	4
vs. Arkansas	W, 62-58	3-7	0-3	2-3	8	5	3	1
E. Illinois	W, 80-68	10-14	5-8	0-0	25	4	5	2
vs. Temple	W, 70-54	5-11	1-5	4-4	15	3	5	0
vs. Missouri	W, 85-70	7-15	3-8	4-6	21	7	5	1
at Memphis	L, 77-74	6-14	5-11	2-2	19	3	3	1
Coppin State	W, 63-37	2-5	2-4	0-0	6	2	1	0
Oakland	W, 88-53	6-11	2-5	0-2	14	5	2	3
at Minnesota	W, 76-70	2-5	1-4	0-2	5	5	3	1
Wisconsin	W, 69-63	2-6	2-3	0-2	6	6	3	1
at Iowa	L, 68-61	2-9	1-6	3-4	8	5	4	1
at Indiana	L, 74-66	6-10	5-7	1-1	18	5	3	1
Purdue	W, 75-62	5-10	1-5	2-3	13	2	4	0
at Penn State	W, 75-63	3-9	1-5	0-1	7	11	6	1
Michigan	W, 67-60	2-10	1-6	0-0	5	5	5	2
at Michigan St.	L, 68-65	5-13	0-4	0-0	10	5	2	2
Ohio State	W, 76-57	1-5	1-4	0-0	3	3	2	1
at Purdue	L, 70-61	2-10	1-6	1-2	6	2	5	2
Michigan St.	W, 70-40	8-13	2-5	6-8	24	5	5	5
vs. Northwestern	W, 73-61	7-11	1-3	3-5	18	5	5	5
Indiana	W, 80-54	5-10	2-3	4-4	16	2	4	2
at Michigan	W, 82-79	4-11	1-5	0-0	9	7	2	3
at Wisconsin	L, 60-59	9-17	2-5	0-0	20	1	5	2
Minnesota	W, 84-60	3-7	1-3	4-4	11	7	1	1
vs. Northwestern	W, 94-65	4-8	2-5	0-0	10	9	2	1
vs. Indiana	W, 73-72	1-7	0-3	4-5	6	7	3	3
vs. Ohio State	W, 72-59	2-11	0-3	0-0	4	5	4	3
vs. W. Kentucky	W, 65-60	6-13	0-3	4-4	16	8	7	2
vs. Notre Dame	L, 68-60	5-14	1-3	3-6	14	3	2	0
TOTALS	25-7	142-327	51-155	49-72	384	159	119	57
		(43.4%)	(32.9%)	(68.1%)	(12.0)	(5.0)	(3.7)	(1.8)

SOPHOMORE YEAR

GREEK TOWN RIGHT UP BROWN'S ALLEY

Guard Thriving Despite Jeers

By Brett Dawson, *The News-Gazette*
JULY 16, 2003

Basketball has taken Dee Brown some places, but Thessaloniki, Greece might be his favorite. It's not just the fun he's having with his teammates at the Junior World Championships. It's not just the chance to play with his friend and Illinois teammate, Deron Williams, for Team USA.

And it's not just the way he torched Lithuania for 47 points Tuesday in an 87-84 U.S. win.

"It's the women, man," Brown said shortly after that performance. "Greek women are so beautiful, and they're everywhere. The city we're in, the ratio is like 13 (women) to one (man). It's unbelievable."

But Brown's been enjoying all the sights. He says even the nonhuman scenery in Thessaloniki, with its waterfront views and ancient architecture, is enough to take your breath away. In all, it's been an almost-perfect trip for Brown. Almost, but not quite.

"I probably could be having an even better time if these Greek people didn't all hate Americans," Brown said. "They see the 12 of us and think we're all President Bush. Like I'm the reason for the war."

Crowds at Team USA's games are decidedly anti-American, Brown said. Or at least they were until Tuesday, when Brown turned their boos to cheers in a performance that might have been his best ever as a basketball player. Brown set five American records for the Junior National team: points, field goals (18), field-goal attempts (29),

Dee Brown dribbles the ball up court as a member of Team USA in its competition against Canada in the Junior World Championships in 2003.
Glenn James/USA Basketball

three-pointers (nine) and three-point attempts (15). And that barely tells the tale of a day in which he outscored the rest of his team by seven points.

"I've been (with USA Basketball) for 13 years, and I don't think I've ever seen anything quite the magnitude of what he did," said Craig Miller, the assistant executive director of communications for USA Basketball. "Especially not in a game that was so tight. This wasn't a blowout. We needed all those points."

against anybody. This was some real competition here."

Lithuania started two guards who both were 6-foot-4 or taller, and the 6-foot Brown said that posed the kind of challenge he expects later in his career, when he hopes to play in the NBA. He also got an up-close look at a more immediate challenge: Lithuanian forward Linas Kleiza. The versatile big man, who will play next season at Missouri, scored 28 points for Lithuania.

"I never get tired of basketball."

–Dee Brown

In fact, Lithuania gave the United States its toughest challenge yet, taking a lead early and fighting down to the wire against Brown and his teammates. But mostly against Brown. Michigan State's Paul Davis scored in the paint with 6:56 to play in the fourth quarter Tuesday, giving Team USA a 71-68 lead. Those two points were the only ones scored by an American besides Brown in the final quarter. The Illini sophomore-to-be scored 21 of Team USA's 23 points in the period, hitting 8 of 9 shots and all five of his three-point attempts.

All that despite playing with a sore knee. Brown banged knees trying to take a charge in a game against Korea. He didn't get the charge. But he put a charge in the U.S. Tuesday in one of the top scoring performances of his life.

"I had a game in high school where I scored 42 and I think I hit 11 (threes) in a row that night," said Brown, the 2001 *News-Gazette* All-State Player of the Year at Proviso East. "And there was an AAU all-star game where I got 70, but that wasn't playing

"Big dude can play," Brown said. "He's going to be a good player."

It's a long time until Brown and Kleiza will meet with their college teams, but Brown will spend much of the time between meetings on the court. He'll return from Greece next week, and then there's a trip overseas with his UI teammates in August.

"I never get tired of basketball," Brown said. "I want to play professionally one of these days, so playing all the time comes with the territory when that's your dream. I'll play anywhere."

He only hopes his next trip features some natives who are more accommodating to their American guests.

"It's hilarious over here when they see all of us black dudes," Brown said. "They'll be like, 'Africa? Are you from Africa?' and we'll say 'No, America. A-mer-i-ca.'

"And then they just stop talking and walk away from you."

ACTION SPEAKS LOUD

Brown's Work Ethic Taking Illini to a Higher Level

By Brett Dawson, *The News-Gazette*
FEBRUARY 20, 2004

It's all in the mannerisms, really. Dee Brown's impression of his coach, Bruce Weber, doesn't rely on the easy target — the Illinois coach's booming voice — so much as the subtleties of Weber's personality.

A way he moves, maybe. A gesture. Brown won't say exactly, and he isn't performing his act — which made waves during a player-performed comedy show two weeks ago at Minnesota — for the media. Not yet, anyway.

But it's a good one. Take it from the subject, who described Brown's dead-on portrayal as "unreal."

"It was hilarious," Weber said. "I even laughed."

More important than Brown's impression of his coach is the impression he's made on him.

Forget Brown's relatively quiet offensive numbers — he's averaging 11.7 points a game and shooting 35.7 percent from the floor — and focus instead, Weber said, on the intangibles he brings to the court.

MOVIN' ON UP

During Wednesday's win against Wisconsin, Weber said, Brown tallied a 10 on Illinois' play-hard chart (which encompasses steals, floor dives, deflections and charges taken) by halftime. Deron Williams was the offensive star against the Badgers, scoring a career-high 31 points, but on a four-point night, Brown had six rebounds, six assists and four steals, all team highs.

"If I compete every night, I don't worry about all that numbers and stuff," Brown said. "It's all

Dee Brown catches his breath during a break in the action at the Assembly Hall. *Mark Cowan/Icon SMI*

about wins. Every night we have a different player step up and have a big night."

And Weber said that isn't just lip service. As much as anyone, he said, Brown has proven willing to sacrifice self for team, a concept Weber considers impressive, particularly from a sophomore the media voted preseason Big Ten Player of the Year.

"He's bought in more than anybody into winning," Weber said. "And that's not easy to do."

Brown is adjusting to life without leading scorer Brian Cook.

"If you had a good freshman year, that means you played a lot," Weber said. "Now your sophomore year, you're going to have to produce more, on most teams."

Including the Illini, who struggled enough early that some experts had them missing the NCAA tournament. Everybody wants to know why.

"I get (asked about) it a little bit," Weber said. "Is it Coach Weber? Is it the offense and him picking

"I don't care about numbers ... it's all about winning to me."

–Dee Brown

Brown admits it can be hard. He looks at Wisconsin's Devin Harris, the pick of Big Ten coaches for Player of the Year honors, and sees a guy who has responded to expectations. The Illinois sophomore admits he probably hasn't, despite ranking third in the Big Ten in assists and assist-to-turnover ratio and eighth in steals.

ROOM TO GROW

The kid they call "The One-Man Fast Break," the brash point guard who's built a reputation as one of the Big Ten's best trash-talkers, said that on a scale of 1 to 10, his confidence is at a 7. For a guy who's typically a 10 playing everything from ping pong to PlayStation, this qualifies as something of an identity crisis.

"It's real low," Brown said. "I need to get back to playing, just having fun. Smile a little bit."

First-year stars who play big supporting parts often struggle, Weber said, when expectations — and personnel — change in their second season.

up the offense? Why is it? And I think it's a little bit of everything."

Is it Brown?

"I tell a lot of people if I was hitting some shots or playing my game, I'd probably be averaging 18, 19, 20 points," Brown said. "But as far as me shooting the ball, I'm not shooting it well this year. I'm not playing the way I know I'm capable of."

Not yet, at least.

"Personally, I don't care about numbers," Brown said. "I can go out there and shoot 18 times and try to chase (Big Ten Player of the Year), but it's all about winning to me."

That's why Brown and his coach now, after a rocky start, are seeing eye-to-eye. And sometimes, Weber's seeing a mirror image.

"We always make fun of each other and do impressions," Brown said. "I'll do (the Weber impression) another day for you, but it's pretty funny, though. I'll show you one day."

Dee Brown reacts to being whistled for a foul during the 2004 Big Ten tournament in Indianapolis.
Robert K. O'Daniell/The News-Gazette

IN GUARDS WE TRUST

That's Illinois' Motto

By Brett Dawson, *The News-Gazette*
MARCH 25, 2004

They share a backcourt and an apartment and an affinity for bowling, and sometimes you wonder if Dee Brown and Deron Williams don't just get sick of one another. Surely, there's some jealousy. Surely, familiarity breeds occasional contempt.

Fights? Shouting matches? Anything? Guys?

"Nope," Brown said. "You're not supposed to get sick of your friends. If you do, they probably aren't your real friends anyway."

And so it is with Brown and Williams, the driving forces behind Illinois' drive to a Sweet 16 matchup Friday against Duke. You want a juicy story? An off-the-record badmouthing? Good luck. The closest you're going to get is the story of

Williams' pet pit bull, who had to vacate the duo's apartment because it wanted to eat Brown alive.

Brown's reaction to this four-legged terror brought upon him by his close friend: "Really, I wish the dog would have liked me so it could have stayed."

Brown and Williams can stuff a stat column — Illinois' two-headed point guard averages a combined 27.5 points, 10.7 assists and seven rebounds a game — but don't expect to see them in a gossip column.

"They complement each other so well," Illinois coach Bruce Weber said. "When the one has a good game, the other doesn't seem to get jealous. It

Dee Brown (left) and Deron Williams walk off the court after Illinois defeated Gonzaga at the John Wooden Tradition in Indianapolis in 2004.
Mark Cowan/Icon SMI

rotates from one to the next. When one's hot, they get him the ball. The next time, it's the other guy."

HOOP AND HYPE

When Weber accepted the Illinois job last spring, he set out to familiarize himself with his team. One of his first stops was the stat sheet, and the season box score thrilled him.

"The first thing I noticed is that Dee and Deron were 1 and 2 in the Big Ten in assists, and I got really excited," Weber said. "Those guys were freshmen. Usually, freshmen want to come in and jack up shots. To see that those guys cared about sharing the ball, it got me excited."

He got even more excited when he got his first glimpse of Luther Head, who at times in the summer and fall — before a string of off-court struggles and suspensions — was Illinois' best guard. Brown and Head have known each other for years, dating to their Chicago days. But it didn't take long for Williams to find his way into their clique when he came to Champaign.

"He's got the kind of personality where he just kind of forces himself in there," Illinois forward James Augustine said. "Some people think he's cocky, but if you're around him, you know he's just a good guy."

And it's the friendship Brown, Head and Williams share, they say, that keeps Illinois' three-guard dynamic dynamite.

"The fans love him, kids love him, old ladies love him. Everybody seems to pick up on Dee."
–Bruce Weber

"I think it's real important, because all the inner workings, what happens off the court and in the locker room is so important," Weber said. "Fans watching, media, coaches, whoever — you know when a team doesn't get along. You can pick up little things."

ON GUARD IN MARCH

Now, Illinois' three-pronged backcourt hopes it can do the things it takes to beat Duke — and maybe to advance to the Final Four. Weber wouldn't count them out.

"(Brown is) the Pied Piper. The fans love him, kids love him, old ladies love him. Everybody seems to pick up on Dee," Weber said. "Deron is more our foundation. He's a rock-solid, old-school point guard/combo guard who knows how to play.

"(Head) gives us another ball handler. At times he can be a scorer. He's more of a slasher than the other two. He can get to the basket. He kind of just takes what the other two don't get, and each game it's a little different."

So far this March, Williams is averaging 15.7 points a game, Brown 15.1 and Head 13.7 — each player at least two points better than his season average. That kind of balance could make Illinois a tough out Friday, even for the mighty Blue Devils and a backcourt that's comparably versatile.

In fact, Brown guarantees Illinois won't get caught with its guards down.

"This time of year, it's all about you leading your troops," Brown said. "That's what guards do. You give us the ball, and we make plays, and I think we can do it just as good as anybody."

Luther Head (left) and Dee Brown congratulate each other near the end of their 72-57 win against Louisville during the 2005 NCAA tournament.
AP/WWP

NO SOPHOMORE SLUMP

Dee Brown's Sophomore Year Recap

By *The News-Gazette*
MARCH 27, 2006

Dee Brown couldn't have asked for a better start to his sophomore year. And, after a rough midseason stretch that saw him battle the first slump of his career, he finished with a flurry, too.

Brown, who starred for USA Basketball during the summer, was named 2003 preseason Big Ten Player of the Year.

"I just want a Big Ten championship," Brown said. "You don't even have to give me any Player of the Year or MVP. Give me another Big Ten tournament championship, give me the conference title, let me go deep in the (NCAA) tournament. You can keep all that other bull."

Brown had 23 points in a season-opening win against Western Illinois and again starred in a Braggin' Rights win against Missouri (18 points, six assists, six rebounds). But Brown and his teammates struggled in first-year coach Bruce Weber's motion offense. After a late-January loss to Wisconsin, Illinois stood 12-5, unranked and buried in the Big Ten standings. But Brown, leading the team in scoring in four games, keyed a 10-0 run to finish the regular season as Illinois won its first outright Big Ten championship since 1952.

Brown and his coach, after a rocky start, began seeing eye-to-eye. After Illinois beat Ohio State 64-63 in the regular season finale, Brown left the court shouting, "I got a ring! I got a ring!"

Brown was coaxed into speaking later in the day by his teammates and Illinois fans at Willard

Dee Brown drives to the basket during the Illini's 72-53 victory against Murray State in the first round of the 2004 NCAA Tournament.
John Dixon/The News-Gazette

Airport in Savoy, where more than 1,000 fans greeted the Illini when they returned home.

"This is one of the best feelings of my life," Brown said, wearing a net around his neck. "The way we came together as a team ... I'm just going to enjoy this."

Brown, who averaged 13.3 points and led the Illini with 51 steals, started every game for the Illini, who finished second in the Big Ten tournament. He was a second-team All-Big Ten pick and an Academic All-Big Ten selection.

In the NCAA tournament, Brown helped Illinois better a higher seeded team (Cincinnati in the second round) for the first in school history, sending the Illini to a Sweet 16 showdown against Duke. Playing 39 minutes with cramps and a stress fracture in his leg, Brown scored 14 points in the Illini's 72-62 loss.

"I knew he was a gamer," teammate Jack Ingram said. "He's got one of the biggest hearts of guys I've played with. I knew he would go as long as he could until the doctors told him to come out."

The injury eventually led Brown to pull out of his 2003 commitment to USA Basketball.

DEE ON HIS SOPHOMORE YEAR

When Coach Self left for Kansas, I took the news a little hard. Almost every school that recruits you is a great school, so I think in a lot of ways you pick a school for the coach. Coach Self was a big reason that I came to Illinois. But I had to adjust and move on. Everybody said I had a beef with Coach Weber, but it wasn't like that. It was just a struggle to learn a new system. I knew that Coach Weber wasn't going to leave. So I had to learn his system. Coming into the season, I was named preseason Player of the Year in the Big Ten, and that put a little pressure on me. I think I came into the season trying to force the issue a little bit, trying too hard to make things happen. But I picked it up at the end of the season, and I moved on from the coaching change. After thinking about it for a long time, I realized Illinois was still a great school, even without Coach Self. We lost a good coach, but they filled his shoes with another good coach.

"I almost cried because I can't play," Brown said. "It's just such an honor and such an experience that you want to keep, but you've got to think long term, and that's what the decision was based on."

"This is one of the best feelings of my life. The way we came together as a team."

–Dee Brown

DEE BROWN'S 2003-04 STATISTICS

OPPONENT	SCORE	FG-FGA	3FG-3FGA	FT-FTA	PTS	AST	REB	STL
W. Illinois	W, 94-66	8-15	4-10	3-3	23	5	2	2
Mercer	W, 93-61	7-13	4-8	0-0	18	3	3	1
at Temple	W, 75-60	6-15	4-9	0-1	16	5	3	0
vs. N. Carolina	L, 88-81	3-17	2-10	0-0	8	3	2	2
vs. Arkansas	W, 84-61	4-12	2-6	3-4	13	6	3	2
vs. Providence	L, 70-51	2-9	0-4	0-1	4	4	4	0
Md.-Eastern Shore	W, 85-43	3-10	1-5	1-2	8	6	0	0
Memphis	W, 74-64	2-11	1-5	0-2	5	7	7	1
vs. Missouri	W, 71-70	5-15	2-7	6-8	18	6	6	2
vs. Ill.-Chicago	W, 75-60	1-8	0-3	2-4	4	9	6	4
Illinois St.	W, 80-73	4-10	2-6	6-8	16	4	2	1
Ohio State	W, 85-63	5-14	2-6	4-5	16	6	3	4
Purdue	L, 58-54	5-15	3-9	1-1	14	1	4	1
at Northwestern	L, 70-60	7-18	5-12	0-0	19	2	6	0
Iowa	W, 88-82	6-12	1-5	1-2	14	8	5	2
Penn State	W, 80-37	3-7	3-7	0-0	9	6	2	1
at Wisconsin	L, 76-56	2-8	0-4	0-0	4	2	3	0
Michigan	W, 67-52	5-11	1-5	2-2	13	2	3	1
at Indiana	W, 51-49	3-9	1-4	0-1	7	3	5	2
at Minnesota	W, 79-69	7-17	2-9	2-2	18	4	1	3
Michigan St.	W, 75-51	3-8	1-3	0-0	7	3	2	1
Wisconsin	W, 65-57	1-4	1-3	1-3	4	6	6	4
at Penn State	W, 66-58	8-13	6-10	2-3	24	5	4	1
at Iowa	W, 78-59	7-14	2-5	2-4	18	10	7	1
Northwestern	W, 66-56	7-10	5-7	1-2	20	2	4	1
at Purdue	W, 81-79	6-13	0-3	3-4	15	3	7	1
at Ohio State	W, 64-63	7-14	4-8	0-0	18	3	6	0
vs. Indiana	W, 71-59	1-5	0-3	0-0	2	4	1	2
vs. Michigan	W, 74-60	6-11	2-6	7-7	21	5	2	3
vs. Wisconsin	L, 70-53	6-12	3-6	0-0	15	1	3	3
vs. Murray State	W, 72-53	8-17	3-8	2-3	21	3	5	2
vs. Cincinnati	W, 92-68	6-12	2-5	0-0	14	8	3	2
vs. Duke	L, 72-62	6-10	2-4	0-1	14	2	3	1
TOTALS	26-7	160-389	71-205	49-73	440	147	123	51
		(41.1%)	(34.6%)	(67.1%)	(13.3)	(4.5)	(3.7)	(1.5)

WHAT DEE MEANS TO ME
Cherished Memories and Lasting Impressions from Illini Kids

Dear Dee,
I'm your No. 1 fan. You and me have something in common. We are good at three pointers. My friend and I played against you. I want the same mouthpiece like you. If you go to the NBA are you going to think about playing with T-Mac? You are the best.

Sincerely,
Khalil T., age 10
Prairie Elementary School
Urbana, IL

Dear Dee,
I love when my family sits down to watch the Illini games. We love when you get close to the basket with the ball. My family starts jumping up (and down) when you do that. Sorry you lost the (last game of the) season, but thanks for being good at it.

Your fan,
Owen M., age 10
Washington Middle School
Monticello, IL

Dear Dee,
You are going to the NBA. Good luck and I wish you the best. Please make a three for me, and I hope you get a very big trophy.

Terell S., age 10
Garden Hills Elementary School
Champaign, IL

Dear Mr. One Man Fast Break,
I am one of your biggest fans. When I grow up I want to be a great player just like you. I played 5th grade hoops for Arcola this year and it was the best. I hope maybe I can see you play in the NBA, and maybe even meet you. You are the greatest, and I hope you get drafted early by a good team. I'll be praying for you and your family.

Best of luck to you,
Anthony W., age 11
Arcola Elementary School
Arcola, IL

Dear Dee Brown,
You are my favorite basketball player on the Illinois Fighting Illini. Could you please dunk it in the NBA because I know that you can. I am told that I am the next Dee Brown.

Nolan H., age 11
Unity West Elementary School
Pesotum, IL

Dear Dee,
I see you on the news and on TV. I like your tattoos. I like the way you shoot three-pointers. Good game.

Sincerely,
Damarco M., age 8
Prairie Elementary School
Urbana, IL

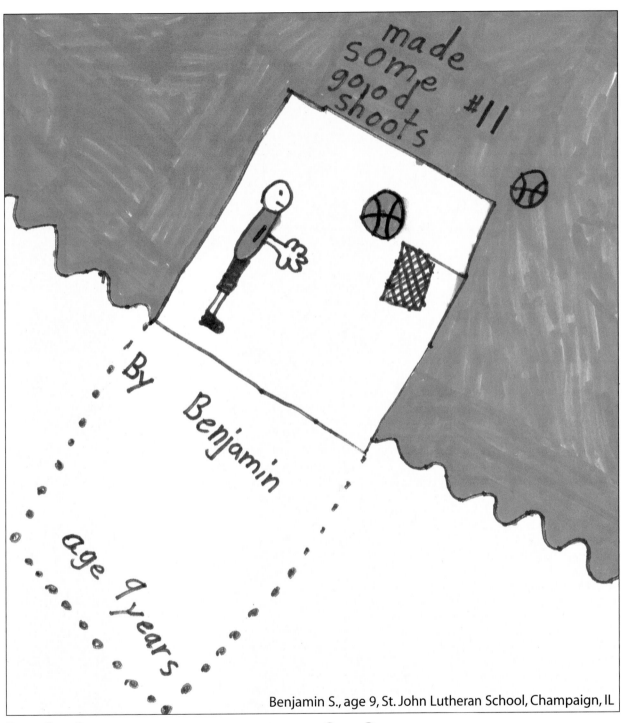

made some good shoots #11

By Benjamin age 9 years

Benjamin S., age 9, St. John Lutheran School, Champaign, IL

Dear Dee Brown,
I have your picture in my video game. You are awesome!

Max S., age 9
Unity West Elementary School
Tolono, IL

Dear Dee,
When we watch Illinois play, I always fight with my dad to "be" Dee Brown.

Nicholas E., age 8
Brimfield, IL

Bailey M., age 9, St. John Lutheran School, Champaign, IL

Dear Dee Brown,
When you were a freshman, you jaywalked in front of my dad's truck. My dad still thinks fondly of that day.

Charlotte W., age 9
Garden Hills Elementary School
Champaign, IL

Dear Dee Brown,
I have you on a poster in my room. I like how you play basketball. I like the way you dribble. I like the way you shoot. Your favorite is three-pointers.

Sincerely,
Tyler W., age 9
Prairie Elementary School
Urbana, IL

Dear Dee,
How are you doing? I want you to go to the NBA so I can watch you again. You should think about going to Cleveland. I played against you and Luther. I was the one who crossed you. I saw you in the mall in Foot Locker. I know you are making a book. I am going to buy it. I hope we get to meet again.

Sincerely,
James C., age 10
Prairie Elementary School
Urbana, IL

Dee Brown,
You are short but you are cool!

Shelby H., age 6
Unity West Elementary School
Tolono, IL

Dear Dee,
I love your game, especially when you are shooting those threes. The last game wasn't fair to me! You have taught me some moves in basketball. My ma starts screaming when you make a shot. My family loves you and your team and we wish you good luck in the NBA.

Erica B., age 9
Garden Hills Elementary School
Champaign, IL

Dear Dee Brown,
I like watching your games. I think you're a pretty good player. I hope you get put in the NBA so I can see you again. I like your orange mouth (guard). I like your braids too. If you come over to my house, my mom will braid your hair. I think your son is cute. Hope I can see you play soon.

Sincerely,
Shawntel H., age 10
Prairie Elementary School
Urbana, IL

Dee,
I hope you're not disappointed that the Illini didn't get as far as last time. You're still the best team.

Your fan,
Andrew R., age 11
Lincoln Trail Elementary School
Mahomet, IL

Dear Dee Brown,
A memory I have of you is when you came to my school and I took a picture with you. I remember when my sister and I were watching the game and the Illini were down by some points. My sister said it was over, but I kept the faith, and the Illini won.

Bryce E., age 10
Garden Hills Elementary School
Champaign, IL

Dear Dee Brown,
You were the best all these years! I really think you would be great for the NBA. I will never forget the saying, "Deeee for Threeee!" You really ruled the court.

Victoria R., age 9
Lincoln Trail Elementary School
Mahomet, IL

Dear Dee,
We live in Waverly, Iowa, where there aren't too many people who wear orange and blue, but that doesn't stop us! We wear our orange "Dee for Three" T-shirts, No. 11 jerseys, and headbands every chance we get. At Christmas, our "Grand" and "Papa" gave us tickets to see the Fighting Illini play at Assembly Hall. What a great time that was! Everyone in the place was wearing orange! It was AWESOME and you put on quite a show! You aren't just a great basketball player; you are a great person, too. We have read stories about how you take time to sign autographs and visit sick children in the hospital. We think that makes you REAL SPECIAL!

GO ILLINOIS!
Tyler (age 12), Eric (age 9),
and Ryan (age 5) W.
Waverly, Iowa

Dear Dee Brown,
You had a good season. I hope you do not break your foot again! I think you and James (Augustine) should go to the NBA. What do you think is going to happen to the Illini next year? Go Dee! Go Illini! Deeeeee for Threee!

Robby C., age 8
Unity East Elementary School
Sidney, IL

Dear Dee Brown,
Me and my friend Sierra love you. We are your biggest fans, and so is my grandpa. You play basketball so good. If you go pro you will be awesome. When we see you on TV it's almost as if you score all the points in the game. Even if you don't win you can always know that we will be cheering for you even when you are not on the court. You inspire us because you never give up and stop trying. If I want to try something and it takes determination and hard work I will always remember you and think if you can do it, I can do it too. Oh yeah, and one more thing, Taylor, Paige, Abbie, Jordon, Andi, Erin, Sara, Shannon and me want to give a big shout out to you. GO ILLINI!

Kaitlyn C., age 10
Paxton-Buckley-Loda Eastlawn Elementary School
Paxton, IL

Dear Dee,
I will remember you because you are a really special person to me and everybody else. You came to my school and you were really nice to everyone. They were really happy to see you, but we had to be quiet because we were too loud and we couldn't hear you talking. You gave us a hug.

Good luck,
Tianna E., age 10
Garden Hills Elementary School
Champaign, IL

I like to watch Dee Brown—the only player anymore that I do watch. I think Dee is fun to watch. He is so good on the court. I am a point guard and how he passes really shows me how to play!

Madison E., age 10
Brimfield, IL

Dear Dee Brown,
I like watching your basketball games. It is fun. I like when the Illini win. I like orange and blue. Blue is my brother's favorite color and my favorite color is orange.

Love,
Danielle S., age 7
Lincoln Elementary School
Monticello, IL

Dear Dee Brown,
What's up? I think you are one of the best role models ever. Even though you're really short you're still really good. Sorry the Illini didn't make it to the Final Four. You still did great this year. Hope you make it to the NBA. You Rock!!

Love, one of your biggest fans,
Kaitlynn S., age 11
Unity West Elementary School
Tolono, IL

A special moment about Dee Brown was when he scored 34 points in the key win over Michigan State (in 2006). He did EVERYTHING: made his shots, hit the threes, made a steal, had some assists and even had some rebounds. Dee had an all around terrific game. I love Dee Brown because he is a great athlete, a great sport, a great student and a great person that I can look up to.

Nathan K., age 11
Wyoming, IL

Dear Dee Brown,
I am very sad that your team was not in the Final Four. I wish you were in the Final Four.

Casey Y., age 7
Unity West Elementary School
Tolono, IL

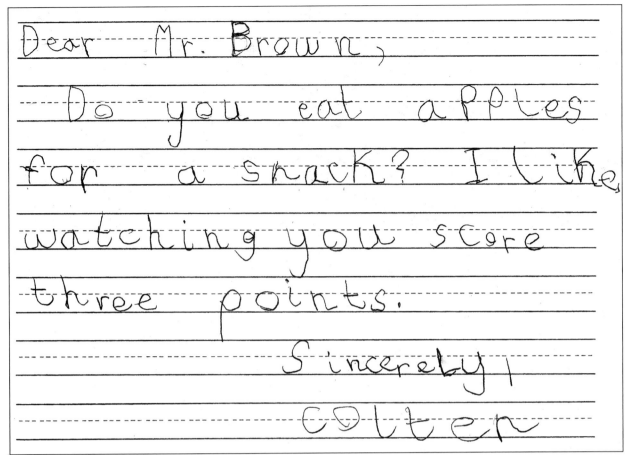

Dear Mr. Brown,
Do you eat apples for a snack? I like watching you score three points.
Sincerely,
Colten

Colton M., age 7, Arcola Elementary School, Arcola, IL

Dear Dee,
You were the best basketball player for Illinois. You did awesome in the tourney, except when you missed against Washington. I come to all your games and support Illinois. I know that you average 14.2 points a game. I bet you're going to be good in the NBA. I will support you.

Your fan,
Sam H., age 10
Lincoln Trail Elementary School
Mahomet, IL

Dear Mr. Dee Brown,
I like the way you play basketball. I watch all of your games. You can dunk very good.

Your biggest fan,
Megan L., age 7
Arcola Elementary School
Arcola, IL

Dear Dee,
How are you? I am fine. I like your braids. They are cute. You bowled against my Dad before the basketball season started. I saw you at the women's basketball games. Me and my sister played (games) with James (Augustine) and you. I like your number because I will be that age next year.

Sincerely,
Tiffany S., age 10
Prairie Elementary School
Urbana, IL

Dear Dee Brown,
You are the best basketball player ever! I wish you could be in the NBA. I will never forget "Deeee for Threee".

Hannah G., age 9
Lincoln Trail Elementray School
Mahomet, IL

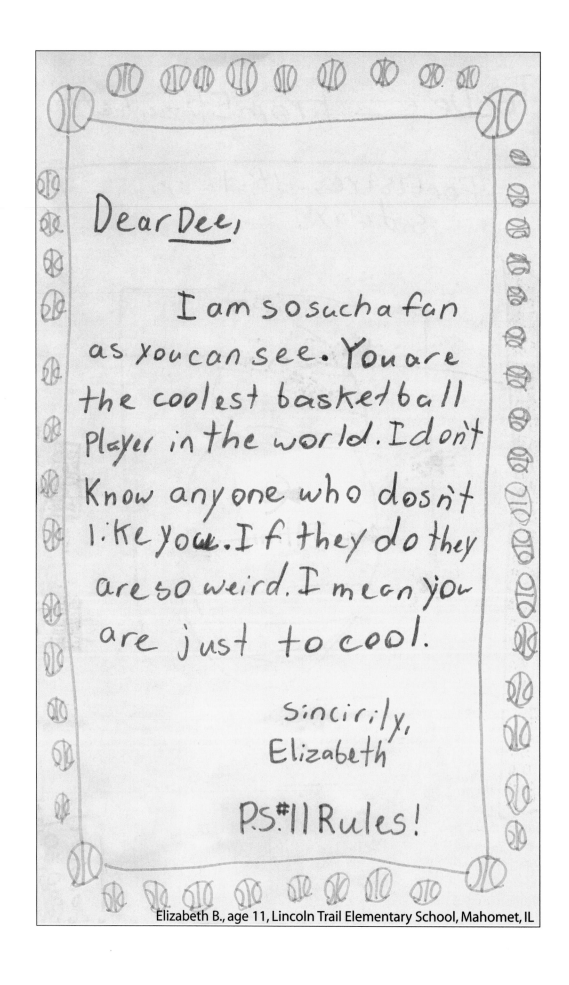

Dear <u>Dee</u>,

    I am so such a fan as you can see. You are the coolest basketball player in the world. I don't know anyone who dosn't like you. If they do they are so weird. I mean you are just to cool.

Sincirily,
Elizabeth

P.S. #11 Rules!

Elizabeth B., age 11, Lincoln Trail Elementary School, Mahomet, IL

Dear Dee Brown,
Thank you so much for playing basketball. You're very fun to watch and are great at the sport. I learned many techniques from you because I play point guard too. You're always a team player, getting assists, and making great shots. Whenever you knock a player over you always help them up. What a great sport! Someday I hope I can be as fast and energetic as you when I play basketball. I can't wait to watch you play in the NBA. Good luck!

Your #1 fan,
Rachel F., age 10
Arcola Elementary School
Arcola, IL

Dee,
Good luck in the NBA. I hope you are on a good team, and whatever team you are on try your best and never give up. I hope you win a lot of trophies.

Javon T., age 10
Garden Hills Elementary School
Champaign, IL

Dear Dee Brown,
I am your No. 1 fan. I hope you make it to the NBA and play on the Rockets. I saw you at the Champaign mall. I remember when you signed your autograph on my piece of paper. I want an orange mouth guard like you.

Sincerely,
Shimaaz I., age 10
Prairie Elementary School
Urbana, IL

Dear Dee Brown,
I like how you make all those shots, and I like basketball too. I wish I could play basketball with you some time. You are better than me. I see you on TV and me and my mom and sister are happy when you make shots. What is cool is that I am 11 and your shirt is 11.

Sincerely,
Denae B., age 11
Prairie Elementary School
Urbana, IL

I like to watch Dee because he is such a good sport and NEVER gives up. My parents always point out how good he is with his team and how he plays with good sportsmanship. He is my hero. I love basketball and want to play just like him out on the court. He is the best player ever!

Mackenzie E., age 12
Kickapoo, IL

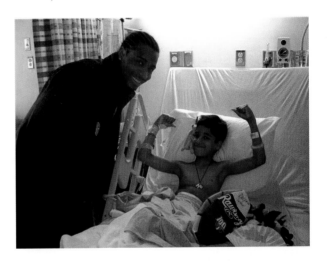

JUNIOR YEAR

BROWN TURNING NBA HEADS

But He's Plenty Happy on Campus

By Brett Dawson, *The News-Gazette*
DECEMBER 20, 2004

There was no one to match his quickness, no ball handler savvy enough to keep him from ripping the rock away. There was no challenge for Dee Brown on Sunday, his 19-point, four-assist, two-steal afternoon leading a 93-56 Illinois rout of Valparaiso in a Las Vegas Holiday Classic game at the Assembly Hall. His challenges came earlier in the week.

"History," Brown said, asked which of his finals gave him the toughest time. "There's so many names to know, so many facts and figures to remember, and it's all essay and written. There's nothing you can do but really focus in and study all night."

If there's one thing Brown can handle, it's focus. A year removed from a slow start to his sophomore season, the Illini guard is playing the best basketball of his life. And with his bachelor's degree "18 or 19 hours away," he said Sunday, it's reasonable to wonder if Brown might be playing his final season in orange and blue.

"We've got a possibility of winning the whole thing or going to the Final Four, so I may get a few looks (from the NBA)," Brown said. "If not, I'll come back."

He'll do it with a degree almost in his grasp. Brown expects to take about 14 hours in the spring semester. That would leave him a few course hours — and an internship — short of a degree in sport management.

Dee Brown launches a shot against Valparaiso on Dec. 19, 2004 at the Assembly Hall. Illinois won easily, 93-56, and Brown scored 19 points.

Holly Hart/The News-Gazette

Asked on Sunday if that makes his return less likely next season, Brown considered the question but didn't commit.

"Honestly, people look at my game or say that they like me, but I really don't feel — I'm not going to say I'm not NBA ready, but as far as being a top pick or being a first-round pick, I just don't see that in my future," Brown said. "I'm playing great basketball, but I don't really see that, so I just try to keep that out of my mind."

For the first time in his career, though, Brown is putting up the kind of All-America numbers that can't help but turn NBA heads. Brown is averaging 14.3 points a game, second only to Luther Head on Illinois' roster, and he's doing it on 8.4 shots a game.

"Dee's energy and good attitude have kind of carried him over," Illinois coach Bruce Weber said after Brown buoyed his top-ranked team to 10-0. "I think (last year) he didn't play with that life, that energy. He joked the other day about feeling sorry for himself for two-thirds of the season."

These days, everybody's talking about Brown, who's becoming a poster child for college hoops. Valparaiso coach Homer Drew was so enamored of Brown that he made a recruiting pitch of sorts. On his way to the postgame news conference, Drew stopped to interrupt Brown's chatter with reporters.

"He's going to play and play and play," Drew said. "And if he doesn't want to play basketball, he could play football, and he'll just flat outrun 'em all down the field. And if he wanted to hit people, he could be on the defensive safety aspect. And if he really got tired of that, he can still play a year at Valpo."

If he plays another year of college at all. Brown always called himself a "three- or four-year" college player. He's never made any secret that he'd like to weigh his NBA options when his junior season ends. But "The One-Man Fast Break" doesn't take study breaks. Even with an eye on his basketball future, his head has stayed in the books.

"I knew a player like me — a short guy — wasn't going to go one and out, two and out," Brown said. "I knew I was going to be able to come in and try to get my degree for my mom."

He promised that to Cathy Brown. And now he's following through.

"It's not easy to do," Weber said. "In the summers, not only is he taking classes, but he's played USA Basketball. A lot of guys seem to get burned out, but he doesn't."

That's because, Weber said, Brown's boundless energy carries over from court to classroom to community service. And it doesn't hurt that Brown doesn't hurt. He's showing no ill effects from the stress fracture that slowed him last season. On Sunday, he once stripped the ball from a Valpo ball handler and streaked downcourt ahead of two Crusaders for a layup and foul.

Brown had a smile and a friendly word for Aris Williams, who hacked him on the play. No surprise there. The Illinois junior is in good spirits on and off the court. Basketball is as good as it's ever been. Brown is shooting 61.9 percent from the floor and 52 percent from three-point range, and his assist-to-turnover ratio is better than 2-1.

And when Cathy Brown calls — as she periodically does — to ask how school is going, her son can report good news.

"I slipped last semester, but I'm trying to keep my GPA above that 3.0," Brown said. "There's nothing like when somebody mentions your name and they can't only mention basketball, they have to say you're a decent student, also."

Brown still is studying the game. The question is whether he'll be taking a crack at history next fall or starting a new chapter of his basketball future.

"If (an NBA team) says ,'Dee we'll take you,' I'll go," Brown said. "But other than that, I love college. My senior year, I want to come back and just have a relaxing internship in the fall, play some basketball and hang out with my buddies."

Dee Brown is all smiles prior to the Illini's 74-59 victory in 2004 against the Georgetown Hoyas in Washington, D.C. Mark Goldman/Icon SMI

BROWNIE POINTS

Guard's Star Power a Sweet Deal for UI

By Loren Tate, *The News-Gazette*
DECEMBER 29, 2004

" Dee for threeee!" is music to Illini ears. And the vibes are sweeping through a newly attentive nation. With a flashy, flamboyant style and a personality to match, UI junior Dee Brown has captured lightning in a bottle. He is riding herd on a stampede that includes 26 victories in the UI's last 28 games. His trademark braids and white headband are copied by youths, wildly popular with his female following and readily accepted among the elders of Illini Nation.

It takes talent to excel, but this story is not exclusively about talent. Arguments can be made in support of several members of the nation's No. 1 basketball team. The UI's smooth-working guards depend on each other. This is about personality, charisma and the ability to uplift more than just a basketball program.

With Brown, there is none of the controversy that clouded the career of backcourt predecessor Frank Williams. And if Cory Bradford drew a nation's attention by draining treys in a record 88 consecutive games, Brown draws a greater audience by making his teammates better.

"Dee has always had that quality," UI publicist Kent Brown said. "And he is very approachable. It helps us immeasurably when a student-athlete enjoys and understands that role."

Wesley Chase (sitting), a 13-year-old boy from Decatur, receives a hug from his mother, Kerry Sprague, after he is overcome with emotion upon meeting Dee Brown (standing). Brown, along with other members of the UI basketball team, visited young patients at Urbana's Carle Hospital on Jan. 10, 2006. It was Chase's wish to meet Brown.
John Dixon/The News-Gazette

"POSTER CHILD"

Standing in the baggage line Tuesday morning at O'Hare International Airport, Dee was hailed by a worker who recognized no one else. Everywhere he goes, people point to him. Dee is the face of this team. Kids see the white headband and want to imitate him. Fans swarm to him.

He is, Mr. Barkley, a role model. And there he was at the Las Vegas airport, signing again and posing for pictures in front of an orange-clad welcoming party shouting, "I-L-L, I-N-I."

Said UI fund-raiser Shawn Wax: "Dee has a magical presence. He emits a pizzazz that transcends youngsters, students, faculty, and fans in general. He is bringing Illini people out of the woodwork."

Wax is in Las Vegas to meet potential contributors, some of whom are traveling from California to see the top-ranked Illini. Wins might not elicit gifts, but a No. 1 ranking doesn't hurt. Brown understands his position in the scheme of things and what it can mean to his future.

"I just try to avoid problems, go to class and give off a positive image," he said. "I love the kids. They are by far the most important. And it's special to get the love of the older fans. I'm just trying to use basketball to my advantage. I grew up around violence on the West Side. A lot of my guys are involved with gangs and drugs. I'm trying to stay out of trouble. I came to Illinois for four years and to graduate."

And perhaps pick up the spirits of the school's athletic department. Illinois has all the enrollment it can handle and was rolling along at a fast basketball pace before Brown arrived. But his impact is no less significant. This is not to say he is more of a perfectionist than gymnast Justin Spring, or more internationally famous than Canadian hurdler Perdita Felicien. But he, more

than anyone else, has put a happy face on an athletic program that is struggling on the football side and, a decade before he arrived, was serving NCAA sanctions about confusing and fan-killing basketball charges.

ROLE MODEL

Brown's first hero was Isiah Thomas, a fellow Proviso East graduate. In his early grades, Dee followed Thomas at Detroit. Dee took Isiah's No. 11 in high school and has kept it at Illinois, that number now the most popular among the community's younger set. But today, in a seemingly conflicting statement, Dee favors the NBA's bad boy, Allen Iverson ... a 76er scoring machine who represents a disrespectful, hip-hop, tattoo-marked, me-first culture NBA officials would like to change.

"Iverson has said and done some things he shouldn't," Brown said. "Once you get a bad image, it's hard to shake. I just take his speed and transition and try to apply it to my game.

"As for the NBA, I don't think my name is talked about much. I'd love to come back at Illinois. My mind-set from the beginning was to play four years. I'm on track. It's going good so far. I have great teammates, and they have helped to make me what I am."

Dee enjoys rap, sometimes improvising in the back of the team bus.

"I like music," he said. "Part of it is lyrics and part of it I make up as I go."

Even old-timers who don't understand it appreciate it. He rolls along as Mr. Feel-Good, gutting it out late last season when his leg was in pain, plugging through a bruised thigh against Missouri last week, laying on the skid marks any time the ball bounces free and ready to erupt on that next must-see fast break. In the big picture,

Dee Brown signs autographs for fans during the Illini's Centennial festivities at the Assembly Hall on Jan. 29, 2005. John Dixon/The News-Gazette

Illinois has never had a more popular basketball player with the fans, not NIU transfer Kenny Battle, not Floridian Derek Harper ... not one more valuable in such a variety of ways.

Now, he isn't just Illinois' poster child anymore. Rashad McCants and Chris Paul must wait their turn as Brown enters 2005 as the face of collegiate basketball. It might not end that way. There are lots of quality players, including some on his own team. But Dee is under a full head of steam, and that's a glorious thing to watch.

BROWN PLAYS IT DOWN

Ever a Team Player, Guard Deflects Praise to Mates

By Brett Dawson, *The News-Gazette*
MARCH 9, 2005

Dee Brown has seen those TV features about poor J.J. Redick. About how the Duke guard is taunted in every visitors' arena. About how Redick is vilified by college hoop fans everywhere.

Brown has seen these stories — and greeted them with a knowing nod.

"I get that all the time, everywhere; you can ask my teammates," Brown said. "I'll get a phone call and just put them on speakerphone so everybody can hear the stuff they're saying."

Of course, nobody hates the guy at the bottom. Brown probably didn't do much to help his popularity Tuesday, when he was named the Big Ten Player of the Year by the league's coaches and by media who cover the conference. It was the capper to an up-and-down regular-season stretch for Brown, who last week graced the cover of *Sports Illustrated* the day before he dropped eight three-pointers on Purdue — then played his worst game of the season in Illinois' first and only loss of the season at Ohio State.

The 6-foot junior, who first heard he won the award from mom Cathy, who called Tuesday morning, said there might come a time when he fully appreciates the trophy. On Tuesday, he was almost disappointed to have won. Not because it's further cause for road-game taunts and phone-call tirades, but because, Brown said, teammates Deron Williams and Luther Head were just as deserving.

"That's just a title — I don't think I'm the best player in this league," Brown said. "I'm just

fortunate enough to be on a good team. Dee Brown is no one without his teammates, without Deron, without Luther, without James (Augustine), without Roger (Powell Jr.)."

The Big Ten didn't leave those guys out. Williams and Head joined Brown — also named defensive player of the year — on the coaches and media first team, and Augustine was a third-team selection by both sets of voters. Powell earned honorable mention on both ballots.

That was a relief for the league's coach of the year, Bruce Weber, who hoped to see each of his players earn some recognition.

"It's Dee's award — he earned it," Williams said. "He played great in the Big Ten season and all year. He deserves it."

The same could be said, Weber pointed out, of any of his three guards, who became the first trio from one team to make the all-conference first team since 1975.

"I think Dee just hit it hot at the right time, right when people were starting to fill out their ballots," Weber said. "If it would've been two weeks before that, it could've been Luther. If somebody really studies it, it easily could've been Deron. But Dee has been very vital in some key wins."

"Dee Brown is no one without his teammates, without Deron, without Luther, without James, without Roger."

–Dee Brown

"I'm pleased for all the kids," Weber said. "I wish Roger would've squeezed in and gotten on one of the teams because I think the best thing about us is that we're a team, and we've had success because different guys have been productive."

Weber's only real concern was that Powell might be disappointed by being the only Illini left off an all-league team, but the coach said his senior and licensed minister "has the most maturity" of anyone on his team and therefore didn't expect a chemistry issue. Nor should he anticipate a problem among his backcourt, said Williams, who was among the first to congratulate Brown when the Player of the Year arrived at Tuesday's practice.

And for all of Williams' and Head's skills, Brown still is the face of the program, the player most loved — and loathed — by observers of Illinois basketball.

But the junior guard, more than willing to absorb all that road venom, was more than happy to deflect praise Tuesday.

"Accomplishments are good to hold onto for the rest of your life, but my goal is just to win — win the Big Ten, which we did, win the Big Ten tourney, win the national championship," Brown said. "I need my teammates to do that. Those guys have done a lot for my game, and I think I've done a lot for their games."

Dee Brown hoists his 2004-05 Big Ten Player of the Year trophy in front of the Assembly Hall crowd.
Robert K. O'Daniell/The News-Gazette

NEARLY PERFECT

Dee Brown's Junior Year Recap

By *The News-Gazette*
MARCH 27, 2006

The conductor for the most magical Illinois basketball season in school history was easy to recognize: He wore a headband, a mouthpiece and a constant smile. Dee Brown's breakthrough junior season coincided with the Illini's run to the NCAA championship game in an electrifying span that neither player nor team will forget.

"Nothing can change how we feel about this season," Brown said after Illinois' 75-70 title-game loss to North Carolina in St. Louis. "We were a team, a family, a bunch of guys that were humble and fought and never gave up. That's how I'm always going to remember this: just a great team and a great group of guys."

The face of college basketball, Brown won awards and respect. The Big Ten Player of the Year — as well as the league's Defensive Player of the Year — was the school's first consensus first-team All-American since Rod Fletcher in 1952. Averaging 13.3 points per game, Brown led the Illini to an NCAA-record tying 37 wins and a No. 1 ranking for 15 consecutive weeks. The run atop the polls started after Illinois beat then-No. 1 Wake Forest 91-73 at a rockin' Assembly Hall.

"We made a statement that we are pretty good," said Brown, who had 16 points and seven assists. "We're one of the best teams, if not the best, in the Big Ten. Hopefully we're one of those teams that are going to make some noise come March."

Brown helped Illinois get off to a school-record 29-0 start in the program's 100th year. He scored his 1,000th career point as Illinois beat Cincinnati

Dee Brown reacts to the sold-out crowd during Illinois' 91-73 defeat of Wake Forest in 2004.
John Dixon/The News-Gazette

to win the Las Vegas Invitational to complete its first perfect nonconference season since 1989-90. Then he effortlessly mingled with hundreds of former Illini watching courtside during the school's Centennial celebration, a weekend highlighted by a win against Minnesota.

"(The reunion) would've been special, but it's even more special now that we're doing good things," Brown said.

He celebrated a second consecutive outright Big Ten title, the team clipping nets after beating Purdue in its home finale. Afterward, he was asked about returning to the Assembly Hall for a possible Final Four celebration.

"It'd be unbelievable," Brown said. "We have to try not to think about that, because thinking about that just gives you the chills. It's gonna be tough, but I think we can do it."

They came close. Illinois won another Big Ten tournament title, cruised to the Elite Eight and dropped Arizona with a hard-to-believe comeback to reach the Final Four. There, it beat Louisville before falling to Carolina.

DEE ON HIS JUNIOR YEAR

When I think about the great year we had in 2004-05, I remember feeling as if we were going to win every game. It seemed like we just couldn't lose. No matter what happened, one guy or a group of guys would make the plays we had to make down the stretch, and we'd pull out a win. It was an amazing year. I had the most fun during my junior year, and it wasn't just about the wins. To me, it was more about the fun we all had together, the chemistry we shared as a team off the court. It was amazing to me that you could have a team be so good and have so many good players and have them all get along so well off the court. Going into the season, Illinois hadn't been to the Final Four in a long time, and getting back there meant a lot to us. It was a great feeling for us to have so much support from so many people across the country. And everywhere we went, we were celebrities. For that year, it was like playing for the Chicago Bulls.

"Of course I'm sad — I'm sad that it's over, that we lost," Deron Williams said. "But we did great things this year. We got to the Final Four. We played for the national championship. Maybe some people who weren't too excited about Illinois basketball are excited now."

"We were a team, a family, a bunch of guys that were humble and fought and never gave up. That's how I'm always going to remember this: just a great team and a great group of guys."

–Dee Brown

DEE BROWN'S 2004-05 STATISTICS

OPPONENT	SCORE	FG-FGA	3FG-3FGA	FT-FTA	PTS	AST	REB	STL
Delaware St.	W, 87-67	5-6	4-5	3-3	17	3	1	0
Florida A&M	W, 91-60	8-10	4-6	0-0	20	4	4	2
Oakland	W, 85-54	2-6	2-5	0-0	6	4	1	0
vs. Gonzaga	W, 89-72	6-10	3-5	2-2	17	8	3	2
Wake Forest	W, 91-73	7-12	2-6	0-0	16	7	6	0
vs. Arkansas	W, 72-60	4-7	2-5	3-4	13	3	1	2
Chicago St.	W, 78-59	5-8	3-6	2-2	15	9	2	2
at Georgetown	W, 74-59	3-9	1-4	0-0	7	6	3	1
vs. Oregon	W, 83-66	5-8	1-3	2-3	13	5	5	3
Valparaiso	W, 93-56	7-8	4-5	1-1	19	4	2	2
vs. Missouri	W, 70-64	4-11	1-5	2-2	11	5	4	3
Longwood	W, 105-79	4-11	0-4	0-0	8	13	2	3
vs. N'western St.	W. 69-51	5-11	1-6	0-0	11	2	2	4
vs. Cincinnati	W, 67-45	4-7	3-6	2-3	13	2	5	3
Ohio State	W, 84-65	5-7	2-4	1-2	13	4	4	0
at Purdue	W, 68-59	4-7	4-6	2-2	14	2	0	1
Penn State	W, 90-64	5-10	5-9	0-0	15	6	1	0
at Northwestern	W, 78-66	5-12	2-6	0-1	12	7	3	1
Iowa	W, 73-68	3-9	1-6	5-6	12	2	1	2
at Wisconsin	W, 75-65	2-9	2-5	2-4	8	5	2	4
Minnesota	W, 89-66	2-6	1-4	2-2	7	6	4	3
at Michigan St.	W, 81-68	7-13	3-6	1-2	18	2	5	3
Indiana	W, 60-47	3-5	3-4	3-3	12	0	3	3
at Michigan	W, 57-51	5-10	2-7	4-5	16	4	2	4
Wisconsin	W, 70-59	5-8	4-6	2-2	16	2	1	1
at Penn St.	W, 83-63	7-11	5-9	0-0	19	11	4	2
at Iowa	W, 75-65	7-11	1-3	3-4	18	3	2	2
Northwestern	W, 84-48	7-10	6-8	0-0	20	5	2	2
Purdue	W, 84-50	9-12	8-10	1-2	27	1	1	0
at Ohio State	L, 65-64	3-11	2-6	5-8	13	4	0	0
vs. Northwestern	W, 68-51	2-4	1-3	0-0	5	2	2	2
vs. Minnesota	W, 64-56	2-12	2-9	4-6	10	0	4	2
vs. Wisconsin	W, 54-43	0-8	0-5	0-0	0	5	3	1
vs. F. Dickinson	W, 67-55	7-10	2-5	3-4	19	2	1	1
vs. Nevada	W, 71-59	0-4	0-3	2-2	2	5	4	0
vs. Wis.-Milwaukee	W, 77-63	7-12	5-8	2-2	21	2	2	2
vs. Arizona	W, 90-89	6-14	3-8	1-2	15	7	5	3
vs. Louisville	W, 72-57	3-10	2-9	0-0	8	4	3	1
vs. North Carolina	L, 75-70	4-10	2-8	2-2	12	7	4	3
TOTALS	**37-2**	**179-359**	**99-228**	**61-79**	**518**	**177**	**104**	**70**
		(49.9%)	**(43.4%)**	**(77.2%)**	**(13.3)**	**(4.5)**	**(2.7)**	**(1.8)**

SENIOR YEAR

Jonathan Daniel/Getty Images

DEE FOR FOUR

Brown Chooses to Lead Young Illini

By Brett Dawson, *The News-Gazette*
JUNE 21, 2005

In his mind, he's always been a point guard. In his heart, he always was a leader. So for Dee Brown, nothing changes. Well, almost nothing.

"My (shot) attempts may go up just a little bit," Brown said Monday after a news conference in which he officially announced his withdrawal from the NBA draft. "That may change just a little."

Otherwise, Brown said, expect more of the same during his senior year: Big plays. Big smiles. Big wins.

In announcing his return to Illinois, Brown wore a smile as apparent as the cast covering his broken right foot. He said he's excited, not disappointed, about having a fourth go-round in orange and blue. He said his issues with Bruce Weber are behind him, and he's focusing on what's in front: recuperating from the broken fifth metatarsal in his foot and returning to lead a young Illinois basketball team back to national prominence.

"It's on my shoulders now," Brown said.

And it's quite a load. Gone are Deron Williams — a likely lottery pick in next week's draft — and probable first-rounder Luther Head. Illinois loses three starters and 48.9 points a game from last season's 37-2 national runner-up. But Brown returns. And for Weber, that's a start.

"Every day, he can show the younger guys and carry them," Weber said Monday. "It's going to be a load for Dee. But I know he loves doing that. He

His right foot in a cast, Dee Brown announces at a press conference on June 20, 2005, that he is withdrawing his name from the 2005 NBA draft to return to Illinois for his senior season.
John Dixon/The News-Gazette

loves to be the guy who gets the other guys to play at another level, bring their games up. It's definitely going to help our program."

Weber, like Bill Self before him, has referred to Brown as the "poster child" of Illinois basketball, a point driven home two weeks ago while Weber was on vacation in Mexico. He walked into a restaurant for dinner and saw a sign at the bar urging patrons to watch Illinois basketball. Brown's picture was on the ad.

As Weber was realizing Brown's international appeal, though, his point guard was trying to get out of college hoops altogether. That same week at the NBA predraft camp in his native Chicago, Brown had designs on leaving Illinois. At least until he broke his right foot — in the opening minutes of his first camp game — and had to put his hoop dreams on hold.

"I was just going in just playing full blast, and whatever they told me in the evaluations hopefully would've been positive and I would've stayed in the draft," Brown said. "Unfortunately, I didn't get to that point."

Still, Brown said, the broken foot wasn't the breaking point in his decision. He talked to several NBA teams even after the injury — the Cavaliers and Clippers among them — trying to gauge his draft status.

"All of them said the same thing: that I didn't move up because of my injury," Brown said. "I wasn't going to be a first-rounder."

And because he hadn't signed with an agent, Brown had options. He considered staying in the draft, even after surgery to put a screw in his right foot. He enrolled in classes at Illinois, returned to Champaign and sometime late last week decided to come back for his senior year.

"I asked my parents, I asked all my family, would they mind another year down in Champaign," Brown said. "And everyone in my family loves Champaign, so I decided just to come back."

Weber is glad he did — and glad Brown didn't let the injury be the only factor in his decision.

"It was not an easy decision for him, and I realize that. Everybody has that dream, and it's right there in front of you, and if you have that opportunity you have to go for it," Weber said. "It's just a shame that he didn't have a chance to finish the Chicago run and see where he stands. But at the same time, he had the smarts to not sign an agent, to keep his options open.

"You gotta give him credit. He listened to people. He listened to his family, NBA people, agents, whoever he could talk to, including our coaching staff."

Brown kept in touch with the Illini staff — Weber included — throughout the process, even after he criticized Weber for "not supporting my decision" to turn pro. That hatchet, Brown said Monday, is long since buried. Weber last week named Brown, James Augustine and Brian Randle co-captains for 2005-06, and Brown said he and his coach have "no beef."

"Y'all get into it with your spouse all the time," Brown said. "You get into arguments with your parents over something. And I know you still love each other. I think our heads are in the same direction. He's a good coach. I wouldn't have come back if I didn't want to play for him."

And make no mistake: A part of Brown always wanted to return to Illinois.

"I really wanted to go pro, and on the other hand, I really wanted to come back and finish my last year because college is fun," Brown said. "I can walk away with my degree in my hand. There was a lot of positives going and staying."

The biggest positives in coming back, Brown said, were that degree — he's taking a required math course this summer and needs an internship this fall to complete a bachelor's in sports management — and the chance to take the reins of what he considers and up-and-coming team.

Dee Brown (center) finds himself in the middle of a huddle with other NBA hopefuls during the NBA pre-draft camp in Chicago on June 8, 2005. *AP/WWP*

"I love challenges," Brown said. "A good basketball player's got to love challenges. I was never afraid to come back to school because Deron was leaving, Luther was leaving, all the top killers were leaving. I was ready for it if I did have to come back."

"I really wanted to come back and finish my last year because college is fun. I can walk away with my degree in my hand."

–Dee Brown

OH, HAPPY DEE

Spartans No Sweat for Brown

By Brett Dawson, *The News-Gazette*
JANUARY 6, 2006

The One-Man Fast Break needed a breather. Drenched in sweat, his face flush, Dee Brown trotted off the court. He turned to a teammate, shook his head and said, "I need some water." It was 20 minutes until No. 6 Illinois' 60-50 Thursday night win against Michigan State tipped off.

"I warm up like that all the time now," Brown said afterward. "Coming out now, I have to do so much. I have to be warmed up and ready to play."

He did it all against the seventh-ranked Spartans, scoring a career-high 34 points and sinking seven three-pointers in a virtuoso performance so captivating, Michigan State coach Tom Izzo likened it to Vince Young's heroics in Wednesday's Rose Bowl.

"It was a Dee Brown night," Izzo said.

It was obvious early, when Brown chucked in a 30-footer up against the shot clock buzzer. And when he threw in a leaning bank shot for a three-point play. And when he faked baseline, shed Spartans point guard Drew Neitzel and then sprinted back to catch a pass from three-point range. He launched, it swished and Brown was at his barking best, giving Neitzel — and anyone else within earshot — the third degree.

"When I came off the screen, (the Spartans) were yelling, like, 'That's off!' " Brown said. "Off? When I hit it, it just sparked something in me. I don't really talk. I just handle business now. When I was young, I used to run my mouth all the time.

Dee Brown is all smiles after sinking a three-point shot in the first half against Michigan State on Jan. 5, 2006. *John Dixon/ The News-Gazette*

Now as you get older, you realize you've just got to go out there and get the job done."

He did some of his best work Thursday. The Illini (15-0, 1-0 Big Ten) played smothering defense, holding Michigan State to 36.2 percent shooting and 26.7 percent from behind the three-point line. They held the Big Ten's leading scorer, Maurice Ager, to nine points, 13 below his average. But with Illinois' offense stagnating — for the first time in 70 games, only one Illini player scored in double figures — Bruce Weber's team needed a catalyst. Brown filled that bill. He made midrange jumpers. He tore downcourt for a one-on-four layup.

"In the last four years, that was probably one of the best offensive exhibitions I've ever seen," said teammate James Augustine, who had seven points and nine rebounds. "I don't know what his shooting percentage was, but it seemed like he didn't miss. We had confidence in him, and he took care of the business."

The theory coming into the season was that Brown would have to handle the business by himself more often. He entered the season an All-American supported by Augustine and a crew of relative unknowns, and it seemed as though Brown would, night in and night out, have to do the heavy lifting.

Instead, Weber said, he has brought his teammates closer to his own level. Even Thursday, with Michigan State (12-3, 0-1) attempting a furious late rally, it was less Brown's scoring than his ability to involve others that impressed Weber. Brown scored only two of Illinois' final 10 points, but he had a hand in virtually all of them.

"I thought a couple of times he could've shot even more, but he was so tired," Weber said. "That's maturity. He makes a great pass to James. He knows he's getting tired, he post-feeds to Shaun (Pruitt), and Shaun hits a big bucket. I'm proud of the maturity he showed with that."

That's the style Brown prefers to play. As a high school star at Proviso East, he shared the spotlight with Michigan State's Shannon Brown, who led the Spartans with 17 points but shot 6 for 16. Dee

Brown had his best season in 2004-05, playing alongside backcourt partners Luther Head and Deron Williams.

On Thursday, Brown took a career-high 22 shots. You might have expected him to do that before Illinois' 15th game of the season.

"I wouldn't do that," Brown said. "It's got to be in the spur of the moment. I wouldn't come out and shoot 20 shots a game. I'm an unselfish guy. I've always been. I need balance. I need another guy that's going to come out here with me and score. But if I get hot, I'm going to continue to shoot."

He got hot against Michigan State. As hot as ever. When he threw in an off-balance buzzer-beater to end the first half — with Spartan defenders "draped all over him," Izzo said — it was clear that this wasn't just another night for Brown.

"All his career, he's been a marquee guy," Weber said. "He loves big games, and obviously he stepped up to the big stage tonight."

Brown didn't know coming in that it would be that kind of night. There was no inkling, he said, as he pushed himself through that withering warm-up, that he was about to light up the Spartans.

It turned out to be a good night for Brown. But as he propped himself against a table for a post-news conference interview, looking more ex-hausted than he had all season, he sounded sincere in saying he doesn't want too many more of them.

"It's fatiguing, and it gets your players not confident in themselves," Brown said. "You can't stand around and watch one player. We're a team, man. Those four letters right there describe Illinois basketball."

Dee Brown is congratulated by members of the Orange Krush after his 34-point effort led the Illini to a 60-50 victory against the Spartans at the Assembly Hall. John Dixon/ The News-Gazette

"It was a Dee Brown night."
–Tom Izzo, Michigan State Head Coach

HANGIN' 11

Should Dee Brown's Jersey Be Retired?

By Brett Dawson, *The News-Gazette*
FEBRUARY 24, 2006

It was in Sweden where Bruce Weber realized that he had inherited not merely a point guard, but a cultural phenomenon. The first-year Illinois coach had taken his team on a get-acquainted trip to Europe, and during a stop in Sweden, a gaggle of girls swarmed Dee Brown.

"There were little girls that had *Slam* magazine with Dee in it," Weber said. "They were like, 'Dee Brown! Dee Brown!' They couldn't speak English, but they knew 'Dee Brown! Dee Brown!' "

That's how far-reaching Brown's impact has been. He's one of the most popular players in Illinois basketball history. He's one of the most recognized college players in the nation. And he's even an international draw. So as Brown prepares to play his final home game Saturday night at the Assembly Hall against Iowa, it's no wonder there

has been some discussion about whether a player with such rare influence deserves a rare honor.

Illinois hasn't retired a number since 1992. Brown's accomplishments have sparked a conversation about whether it's time to do it again.

"Oh, man, it would be an incredible honor," Brown said. "I mean, there have been so many great players here, and for them to even consider that would just be crazy."

They have considered it. Don't expect Illinois to raise No. 11 to the rafters during Saturday's Senior Night festivities. But it's safe to assume that Brown's is a common name in an ongoing

Dee Brown, surrounded by friends and family including his mother and son, stands behind his framed jersey during Senior Night festivities at the Assembly Hall. Robin Scholz/The News-Gazette

conversation about honoring Illinois basketball tradition.

"He's become national, his face, his smile, the No. 11, the braids, the headband," Weber said. "And besides the pizzazz and the personality, he's backed it up with numbers, also.

"You're talking about one of the leading scorers in the history of the school. You're talking about assists, steals, three-pointers — there's so many categories that he's up there. I think it would be a good place to start (retiring jerseys), especially in recent history."

SELECT COMPANY

No Illinois basketball player ever has had his jersey or number retired. Only three Illini athletes — football greats Red Grange and Dick Butkus and baseball legend Lou Boudreau — ever have had their numbers retired. But Weber wants that to change.

"You're not going to retire the number and no one could use it again," he said. "You retire the jersey with the guy's name. I think that would be a possibility."

Weber wants a physical representation of Illinois' basketball tradition at the Assembly Hall. The Illini have raised banners for team success and for the All-Century basketball team announced last season. Weber's goal is to add individual jerseys into the mix.

"I think that would be something that would add value to the building," former Illinois point guard Bruce Douglas said. "As long as the motivation is to build the tradition and to create a bond between generations, I don't think anyone would have a problem with that."

Former players, Douglas said, would likely be near-unanimous in their praise for the decision to recognize the past.

"I would say to you that retiring numbers is something that you can build some real history on," former Illini Jerry Colangelo said. "I think it's something to really consider. Dee Brown would be a terrific candidate."

STATING A CASE

Brown isn't campaigning to have his jersey raised to the roof. Just the opposite, in fact.

"It's crazy that people even think about it, man," Brown said. "Just for them to talk about it, that's just unbelievable. It's humbling. I mean, I never expected anything like this to come to me to where people would even discuss that."

Brown's face has adorned countless magazine covers. He's been a fixture on ESPN television promos. And his signature look — headband, braids, orange mouthpiece — has inspired a generation of wannabes from Champaign to Sweden. Brown speaks to school kids. He visits sick children in the hospital. He earned his Illinois degree in 3 1/2 years. Sometimes he seems too good to be true.

"Besides being the poster child for Illinois, I think he's really been the poster child for college basketball," teammate Brian Randle said. "Being here for four years, leading so many teams, doing so many great things for this university, both on and off the court ... I think it would be very fitting (to retire his jersey)."

Those closest to the situation say Brown's signature on the program needs no further analysis.

"I don't think anybody will ever do as much for this program as he's done or be as big as he's been to this program," said freshman Chester Frazier, Brown's point guard backup. "When you even think of Illinois, you think Dee Brown. That's nationally known. You gotta retire his jersey."

To many Illini fans, Dee Brown played the part of Superman on several occasions throughout his Illinois career. *Darrell Hoemann/The News-Gazette*

CARRYING THE LOAD

Dee Brown's Senior Year Recap

By The News-Gazette
MARCH 27, 2006

Coming back to Illinois for a senior season was a hard decision for Dee Brown. Making sure Illinois kept winning on his watch was the hard part.

"People don't care that we lost players," Brown said. "They're going to come at us. You know how they always say college basketball is about the name on the front of the jersey? They'll just see that it's Illinois, and they're going to come to play. We're elite now, like Duke or North Carolina. Now we have to stay up on that level."

Brown made sure the Illini did just that, finishing his career tied with James Augustine as the winningest players in school history. The Illini recorded their second consecutive unbeaten nonconference season and challenged for the Big Ten title until the final week of the season.

Along the way, Brown was named first-team All-Big Ten for the second consecutive year.

"Dee has had his time in the past as a first-team guy and even the Player of the Year, and if we win a couple more games, he has a great chance to have been Player of the Year again," Illinois coach Bruce Weber said.

A preseason Wooden Award candidate, Brown helped the Illini to a 15-0 start. Included in the run was a fourth consecutive Braggin' Rights win against Missouri. Brown finished his career averaging 16.8 points a game against Mizzou.

James Augustine (left) and Dee Brown leave the court together after the Illini's 70-58 victory against Indiana on Feb. 19, 2006. The seniors came in to the program together, and left together as career leaders in wins with 114.
Daniel Williams/The News-Gazette

"I'm going to miss this game, to be honest with you," Brown said.

Climbing a host of school career charts, Brown almost single-handedly kept the UI's homecourt win streak alive with 34 points against Michigan State and 26 against Michigan.

"We started with a difficult Big Ten stretch, but it's good for us. It's going to be a grind," Brown said. "We've got a big 'X' on our back, but we just feel like if we go out there and play Illinois basketball and continue to believe, (we'll be fine). There's a lot of basketball left."

A home loss to Penn State would eventually prevent Illinois from catching

DEE ON HIS SENIOR YEAR

For me, my senior year was interesting, because I had to go out and play with a lot on the line personally. Obviously there was a lot at stake for me in terms of my basketball career. It was also my last chance to play with James Augustine, who I had been playing with since AAU ball before I got to college. James is like my brother, and he always will be. I also felt responsible for bringing the young guys along, to get them ready for the future. I wanted Illinois to send a message that we're not some flash-in-the-pan program that was going to go 16-15. We're always going to be a contender. Coach Weber always says a season is about how you finish, and obviously it was a disappointment to lose in the second round of the NCAA tournament. But on the whole, I felt like we had a great year—a lot better than many people expected of us.

"We're elite now, like Duke or North Carolina."

–Dee Brown

Ohio State for the regular season title. Illinois lost in the first round of the Big Ten tournament and the second round of the NCAA tournament, when Brown's last-second three-pointer rimmed out against Washington. It was fitting that Brown — who ranks in the top three in 10 UI career categories including scoring, three pointers made, assists, steals and games started— would take the final shot.

"It was a good shot," Brown said. "I usually make it."

Brown finished his senior year with a string of accolades. He was named First-Team All-Big Ten by both coaches and media for the second consecutive year. He also won the Cousy Award, given to the nation's top point guard; the Frances Pomeroy Naismith Award, given to the nation's

best player 6 feet and under; and was selected for the John Wooden All-American team.

Brown won 114 games at Illinois and two outright Big Ten titles, taking fans on an unforgettable four-year ride.

"I get so much love here, it's humbling," Brown said. "I get nervous when I think about what would've happened if I'd gone to another school. When I think back on it, it came down to, like, the last 30 seconds for me between Illinois and Michigan State. I could've gone either way. And now? The academics, the people, the basketball program, the alumni, the way people show me love — I can't imagine what it would be like if I went somewhere else."

DEE BROWN'S 2005-06 STATISTICS

OPPONENT	SCORE	FG-FGA	3FG-3FGA	FT-FTA	PTS	AST	REB	STL
S. Dakota St.	W, 90-65	6-16	3-8	4-6	19	2	1	3
Texas-Pan Am.	W, 71-59	7-17	5-13	1-2	20	4	7	4
Texas Southern	W, 93-59	5-11	3-8	1-1	14	5	6	1
vs. Wichita St.	W, 55-54	3-14	2-9	0-2	8	5	2	3
vs. Rutgers	W, 77-57	4-7	0-2	2-2	10	4	2	0
at N. Carolina	W, 68-64	6-19	0-6	2-3	14	3	0	2
vs. Xavier	W, 65-62	4-16	3-10	9-10	20	7	5	3
Ark.-Little Rock	W, 75-49	2-8	1-5	1-2	6	10	5	1
Georgetown	W, 58-48	5-16	2-7	4-5	16	3	3	0
vs. Oregon	W, 89-59	9-15	5-8	3-4	26	7	4	1
Coppin State	W, 61-42	2-7	2-6	2-2	8	7	2	0
vs. Missouri	W, 82-50	5-11	4-7	3-5	17	7	4	2
SE Missouri St.	W, 89-64	6-17	3-9	1-1	16	5	2	0
Tenn.-Martin	W, 84-46	2-5	1-2	0-0	5	10	1	2
Michigan St.	W, 60-50	12-22	7-13	3-3	34	3	1	2
at Iowa	L, 63-48	2-13	1-10	1-2	6	3	2	3
Michigan	W, 79-74	6-17	5-10	9-10	26	5	2	1
at Indiana	L, 62-60	1-9	1-6	2-2	5	11	5	3
at Northwestern	W, 58-47	6-10	2-5	4-6	18	8	2	2
Minnesota	W, 77-53	7-11	3-6	0-0	17	5	4	1
Purdue	W, 76-58	5-14	0-5	2-3	12	9	4	1
at Wisconsin	W, 66-51	6-18	1-5	3-6	16	7	4	2
Penn State	L, 66-65	3-12	3-11	2-2	11	4	3	0
at Ohio State	L, 69-53	5-13	2-5	0-0	12	3	3	1
Northwestern	W, 63-47	6-14	2-8	2-2	16	4	3	2
Indiana	W, 70-58	3-12	1-6	3-4	10	4	5	0
at Michigan	L, 72-64	8-19	3-8	1-1	20	6	1	1
Iowa	W, 71-59	2-12	2-9	0-2	6	9	2	0
at Minnesota	W, 71-65	5-14	2-9	2-2	14	4	1	3
at Michigan State	W, 75-68	6-13	5-10	3-4	20	4	2	2
vs. Michigan State	L, 61-56	2-10	1-5	0-1	5	7	5	1
vs. Air Force	W, 78-69	1-7	1-6	5-5	8	10	8	4
vs. Washington	L, 67-64	5-18	2-6	3-3	15	6	1	2
TOTALS	26-7	157-437	78-243	78-103	470	191	102	53
		(35.9%)	(32.1%)	(75.7%)	(14.2)	(5.8)	(3.1)	(1.6)

THE IMPORTANCE OF GRADUATION

By Dee Brown

In my time at Illinois, I always tried to represent the true meaning of the word "student-athlete." I hope that my legacy here at Illinois is one of a player who always played his hardest and gave his all, but also one of a guy who achieved good grades. The academic side of my college career is important to my family, and a big part of who I am as a person.

I'm a competitor, and that always has extended beyond just basketball. I want to win at any game I play, but I also want to do well in school. I hope that I've represented the word student as well as the word athlete. Just as I think my play on the court speaks for itself, I think my grade point average speaks for itself.

As a player, my greatest fear has always been injuries. Last year, I had to face that, when I broke my foot at the NBA predraft camp. But now that I have my college degree, I know that I'll always have options. When basketball isn't there for me anymore, I can pursue other things.

When I was younger, I was often told, "Basketball can be taken away from you, so get your education." I did that. My degree from the University of Illinois—one of the best universities in America—is something that nobody can take away from me. To have my degree is something I really treasure.

No one in my family other than myself has ever graduated from college. For me to be the one who grew up to become something big—a college graduate—is special to my entire family. It means a lot to me.

Of course I could never have achieved this without God's support. And I owe so much to my family, my mom especially. They pushed me to succeed not only in basketball but academically as well, and I'm grateful to them for that, always.

Dee Brown shares a laugh during the filming of a television commercial at the UI Main Library.
John Dixon/The News-Gazette

WHAT DEE MEANS TO ME

Cherished Memories and Lasting Impressions from Illini Nation

"That charismatic smile that he always had off the court. You could not ask for a better ambassador for the University of Illinois and Illinois athletics."

–JOSH MEANS, WHEELING, IL

"He made basketball fun for me!"

–MEGAN LOISELLE, LINDENHURST, IL

"My favorite memory of Dee is the 2005 game at Michigan where he stole the ball twice and brought the team back to win the game and keep the undefeated season going. I-L-L-D-E-E."

–TERRY HIATT, PARIS, IL

"My favorite memory is Dee walking out of the tunnel on Senior Day at the Assembly Hall carrying his young son. A great picture of father and son. The headband and high socks. We will miss him and the excitement he brought to each game and the team."

–CHRIS TUCKER, SIDNEY, IL

"Dee was the orchestrator of the shirt-poppin', school-proppin' craze that every college basketball player in the nation exhibited after a game-changing play during the season of 2004-05. He made it popular and everyone followed him."

–ANDREW PYLE, CHAMPAIGN, IL

"The socks. The headband. The energy. The leadership. The Orange."

–RYAN MCDEVITT, OREGON

John Dixon/The News-Gazette

"Numerous times seeing Dee steal the ball out front with just a swipe, knocking it away and he's off to the races. That is classic Dee."

–TERRY POWELL, DANVILLE, IL

"Besides Dee's contagious smile, I will never forget the "DEEEEEEEE FOR THREEEEEEEE," and how fast he could get down the basketball court. Also I won't forget how he could get the fans cheering loudly for the Illini. Good luck Dee, in whatever you do."

–RUTHIE BURBERRY, MAHOMET, IL

"My favorite memory of Dee is the way he presented himself on and off the court. My 6-year-old loves Dee and is in love with basketball because of Dee. Dee's smile just brightens up the court. My son's smile when watching Dee play either on TV or in person brightens my day. I am not sure what my son will do next year without Dee being on the court. Watching Dee's mother at the games is also exciting. She just beams with pride. Thanks for the memories Dee. You are Illinois basketball to us. We will miss you."

–AMY BLEDSAW, WARRENSBURG, IL

"I have a grandson, Murphy McCool, that at 14 months old can say just a few choice words, but let me tell you he can say, "Dee Dee, Shoot the Ball." Good luck Dee in your future, wherever it takes you."

–PAT MENGES, DANVILLE, IL

John Dixon/The News-Gazette

"I am an employee at Carle Clinic, and when Dee Brown made an appearance here, he touched the lives of many of the young children, some of whom may never get to cherish an experience like this again. Good luck to the future of Dee Brown."

–HALEY COSTELIC, BROADLANDS, IL

Mark Cowan/Icon SMI

" The greatest memory for me was when I saw Dee in my son's school here in Champaign and Dee was talking openly to the eighth-graders about how important it is not only to be a great athlete, but most importantly to be a great student, to stay in school and stay off drugs. My son has looked up to Dee as an example in his life, and Dee's influence off the court in the community is just as important as what he's done on the court. "

–DEBBIE CLARK, CHAMPAIGN, IL

" The picture in *The News-Gazette* when Dee Brown visited the very sick little boy who had always dreamed of meeting Dee will always be something that stands out in my mind. It shows the type of person Dee was off the court. The picture of the mother embracing her son who was overwhelmed when he got to meet Dee is priceless! "

–DIANNE MURPHY, ARCOLA, IL

" My favorite Dee Brown moment was meeting him and finding that he is completely humble and genuine. He is so much more than an athlete — he was a dedicated, serious student graduating early with a 3.05 GPA, a loving and proud father, devoted son, and committed community serviceman. Dee has shown so much heart and character throughout his collegiate career, so thank you Dee for being you! "

–ERIKA WEAVER, MATTOON, IL

" Dee Brown is a great role model for all young and old Illini fans. He was a joy to watch on the court and he was a great man off the court. You always hear someone talk about how they met Dee at a restaurant, a ladies Illini game, at the mall, stopping by the schools or the hospital to see our future leaders. Dee always remembers his fans. Thanks for all you have done. We will miss you next year, both on and off the court. "

–AMY MARTIN, CATLIN, IL

" My most memorable Dee Brown moment is from the Wake Forest-Illinois game on December 1, 2004. The image of Dee, decked out in the orange Illinois uniform, orange headband, and orange mouthpiece, sitting on the court of the Assembly Hall, smiling and nodding to the cameras as the Fighting Illini were humbling then No. 1-ranked Wake Forest, is vintage Dee. That moment was a harbinger of a special basketball season! "

–JAN SCOTT, URBANA, IL

Heather Coit/The News-Gazette

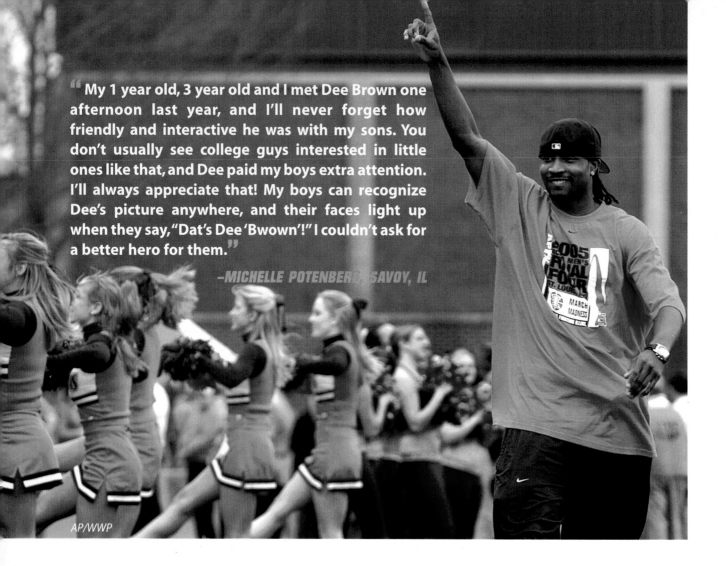

" My 1 year old, 3 year old and I met Dee Brown one afternoon last year, and I'll never forget how friendly and interactive he was with my sons. You don't usually see college guys interested in little ones like that, and Dee paid my boys extra attention. I'll always appreciate that! My boys can recognize Dee's picture anywhere, and their faces light up when they say, "Dat's Dee 'Bwown'!" I couldn't ask for a better hero for them.**"**

—MICHELLE POTENBERG, SAVOY, IL

AP/WWP

" There are so many memories I have of Dee Brown, but the one I will remember for a very long time is the last home game. Dee and James were sitting on the bench and Dee put his arm around James, they both smiled because it was the final game for them at the Assembly Hall. Thanks for the memories.**"**

—LINDA KNOX, CHAMPAIGN, IL

" The March 24, 2006, *Chicago Tribune* reported that "The University of Illinois in Champaign received a record number of applications this year at 22,300. That's 12 percent more than last year." And I think Dee Brown is one of the biggest reasons for this increase. He really is the best thing that's happened to UIUC in a very long time!**"**

—NORMA MILLER, CHAMPAIGN, IL

" My husband and I passed Dee in Memorial Stadium during halftime of the homecoming game last year [2005]. He walked right by me. "Is that Dee Brown?" I said. We turned around, and so did he. He smiled at us — that beautiful Dee smile — even though all we could do was make unintelligible noises of delight at running into him. I was impressed that he took notice of us and responded, even though he must get that kind of greeting a lot.**"**

—RACHAEL MCMILLAN, CHAMPAIGN, IL

" Dee's optimism is as unquenchable as his smile! After his injury at NBA camp crushed his dream last summer, he could have quit, sulked through this season, or become bitter. He's always looked on the bright side of life, of other people (fans, teammates, opponents, and media), of fame, of basketball, of school, of practice, of leadership, of hard work—of everything. That's not something many of us choose to do, but he does it so naturally. Dee is my compass for being a positive, humble, grateful person."

–SANDRA BURT, CHAMPAIGN, IL

" I remember the night we ate at the Ribeye in Champaign and the team came in to eat before they left town for a game. My husband and I were spell-bound just watching all of them, but Dee had a smile for everyone who spoke to him. He has been such a sportsman for the U of I and also a man to be looked up to in Champaign-Urbana. We are proud to say we will always remember Dee Brown wherever his paths may go from here. I have his autograph and many magazines with articles about him that we will cherish forever and will be passed on to our grandchildren."

–PEGGY STACY, CHAMPAIGN, IL

" Dee is a great basketball player and his love of the game makes him so much fun to watch on the court. But my best memory of Dee Brown happened last season [2004-05] at the Las Vegas tournament. We got to the game early and my husband and son sat right behind the bench for the first game of the tournament. My son was thrilled and cheered loudly throughout the game. As the game ended he went to the end of the bench as the players were leaving the court and stuck out his hand to get high-fives. They all gave him five. Dee gave him five and walked to the locker room. At the door, he turned around, came back, took off his headband and gave it to my son. He said, "Here, you take this." My son was speechless. Dee became an even bigger hero in his mind. My son loves sports—especially basketball and football. He is a fierce competitor but has Down syndrome: He experiences the thrill of being a basketball player through others. Dee was not asked to do anything and there was no camera for publicity. He came back and gave my son that headband out of the kindness of his heart. I don't think many college basketball players, whether or not a star, would have done the same thing."

–NANCY ERICKSON, ALTONA, IL

" I'll always remember the love Dee showed to our grandson, Will Tate. He e-mailed Will, signed shirts and posters for Will, and then came to visit him in the hospital and played poker with him even as Will was very sick. When Dee found out Will had died, he called the family to tell them how sorry he was. He is a real class act, friendly and outgoing, and I have enjoyed watching him play for the Illini."

–MARY HACKL, CHAMPAIGN, IL

DOUBLE-ONE FOR THE AGES

The Legacy of Dee Brown

By Loren Tate, *The News-Gazette*
MARCH 27, 2006

Like any rock star, Dee Brown drew doubters and critics during his basketball career. He met the full brunt of opposing defensive strategies this past season. And at times the basket moved on him as though in shifting winds. One Chicago call-in show brought an "overrated" charge up for debate. NBA scouts remain undecided whether he is a "true point guard" and worthy of first-round consideration.

And then there was *Sports Illustrated*. In one issue Brown found himself atop a list of point guards "with the chops to negotiate 75-possession track meets and (also) grind it out slugfests." After the 2006 NCAA's first two rounds, that article was followed by with a "most disappointing" list featuring Dee Brown alongside Michigan State's Shannon Brown, Indiana's Marco Killingsworth,

Kansas' Brandon Rush and North Carolina's Keyshawn Terry.

Win or lose, the 6-foot Illini speedster always was in the eye of the storm.

But if you're seeking his true value, ask yourself two questions: (1) What would this 26-7 Illini team have accomplished if Dee had turned pro early, and (2) how will next year's team survive without him? And then consider his monumental four-year contribution in which he became, in the words of *News-Gazette* beat writer Brett Dawson, "a cultural phenomenon."

Illinois never has produced a more popular, inspiring and courageous basketball player. That honor had been held by Kenny Battle since 1989, when Illinois reached the Final Four with a "Battle

Dee Brown tugs at his jersey in a move that he popularized throughout college sports. *AP/WWP*

warcry. But if Battle was the most [...]t dunker on a team of dunkers, he [...]e best player on that team. Nick Anderson [...]And Battle never approached the national [...]ognition attained by Brown when he sparked a [...]7-2 team to the 2005 title game.

Brown was *The Sporting News* 2005 Player of the Year even though the NBA recognized his running mates, Deron Williams and Luther Head, as superior talent worthy of the draft's first round. Brown finished third in voting for the Wooden Award and was the UI's first consensus All-American since Rod Fletcher in 1952.

In the modern TV era—the post-Whiz Kids, post-Eddleman, post-Kerr period—the UI never

freshman, he deposited two free throws at :01.9 to ice a 62-58 win. Later that year, in an 82-79 defeat of Michigan, his 12-footer at 1:20 gave Illinois the lead for good. And he was the driving force in the 65-60 NCAA win against Western Kentucky with 16 points and two free throws at :22.8. As a sophomore, he notched the final free throws to create a four-point lead in a 71-70 win against Missouri. At Penn State, with the Nittany Lions smelling upset, he sank six incredibly long treys in a 24-point outburst. Most memorable in 2005 were his three steals that rallied the Illini to a 14-3 run and the comeback victory at Michigan. That brief spurt, more than anything else, earned Brown the Big Ten Defensive Player of the Year award.

"[Dee Brown is] a cultural phenomenon." –Brett Dawson, News-Gazette writer

had a basketball player as prominent on the national scene. His braids, headband and jersey No. 11 have graced magazine covers and metropolitan newspapers from New York to Los Angeles.

He played more minutes than any Illini in history, joined James Augustine in posting an Illini record 114 wins, and posted career totals that left him second to Cory Bradford with 299 three-pointers, second to Bruce Douglas with 231 steals and 674 assists, and third in points with 1,812 behind Deon Thomas (2,129) and Kiwane Garris (1,948). Perception being a part of reality, Dick Vitale placed Brown directly behind the nation's 1-2 scorers, Adam Morrison of Gonzaga and J.J. Redick of Duke, as the nation's premier clutch shooters.

Actually, Brown never hit a game-winning basket at the buzzer although, with Illinois down a point to Wichita State in late November, the Shockers turned Warren Carter loose for the winner by double-teaming Brown. Such was his value. And that is not to say he didn't make clutch plays along the way. Against Arkansas as a

But it was against Michigan State that Brown attained super-hero status. Bill Self's 2003 team had lost at Michigan State before the Spartans came to the Assembly Hall, and the freshman guard racked 24 points with five assists, five steals and five rebounds in a remarkable 70-40 rout. That was the start of Illinois' five-game win streak against Tom Izzo's athletes. Brown later erupted against the Spartans with a career-high 34 points during his senior season in a dazzling long-shooting exhibition at the Assembly Hall.

This was followed, ironically, with his weakest effort at Iowa where he even missed layups (he made 2 of 13 shots) in a 63-48 loss. From a shooting standpoint, that's the way he senior season went, up one day, down the next. Having missed 14 weeks of summer work due to a fractured foot, he started slowly. He was 19 for 68 on treys (28 percent) through the first nine games, and never fully recovered. In Illinois' seven losses, he shot the same 28 percent on three-pointers. After posting gaudy percentages of 43.4 from the

Luther Head (left), Deron Williams (center) and Dee Brown share a laugh as the Illinois basketball team is welcomed home at Memorial Stadium following the team's 2005 NCAA Final Four run. Will these three be remembered as the greatest backcourt in Illinois history? *Robin Scholz/The News-Gazette*

arc and 49.9 overall a year ago, he dipped to 35.9 and 32.1 in his final season.

"With teams locking in on him, and his added responsibilities at the point, Dee's shooting slipped," coach Bruce Weber said. "He had to take a lot of bail-out threes against the shot clock.

"Dee was always a part-time point, but the full-time job takes a toll. It's like being a quarterback in the NFL. Still, he got us a lot of wins (26) with a new, different mix of players.

"We never got into our offense as quickly as we should. We didn't have the skilled passers and playmakers alongside him."

Whatever his shortcomings, Illini Nation won't soon forget the sight of Dee Brown pushing the

basketball, outracing an opponent for a driving layup, demoralizing Izzo with spectacular plays, going undefeated in Chicago's United Center and against Missouri, winning two undisputed Big Ten titles, and helping Illinois to No. 1 status during the bulk of a 37-2 season.

He was the central figure in mobilizing the largest contingent of orange partisans ever seen in these parts. Illini Nation followed Brown and the Illini from coast to coast. If they were given the vote, his No. 11 would be hanging high in the Assembly Hall.

For certain, Dee Brown will be a tough act to follow.

CLOSING THOUGHTS

By Bruce Weber, UI Men's Basketball Coach

Before I came to Illinois, I knew about Dee Brown. I had seen him play his freshman year, and I had heard stories about his speed. But you had to see it to really understand it. I remember that when we took our European trip the summer I took the Illinois job, there was a play where a ball got tipped and Dee was running one-on-five down the court. And he still got a layup.

It was also on that trip when I came to understand the phenomenon that is Dee Brown. There were girls in Sweden with copies of *Slam* magazine that included a story about Dee. They shouted to him: "Dee Brown! Dee Brown!" They didn't speak English, but they knew Dee Brown. I don't know how Dee came up with the idea of the braids, the headband, the mouthpiece, the socks—all of those things that have made him such a recognizable figure. But he thought of all of that. We're in an age where there's intense media interest in college basketball, and Dee has fed off that.

I've kind of jokingly called Dee the "poster child of Illinois basketball," but that's what he has become. There always has been a guy—whether it was Kenny Battle or Kendall Gill, or Johnny "Red" Kerr back in the 1950s—that people always talked about when they thought "Illinois basketball." I think Dee passed all of them up during his career. He put himself on top of the list. When you think Illinois basketball, you think Dee Brown.

More than that, he became the face of a lot of what's positive about college basketball. He made good grades. He really finished all his classwork in three years. He did community service to the max. And I believe he became a sort of hero to little kids everywhere. Even if you aren't going to grow to be over 6 feet tall, Dee Brown has given you an example you can look up to. A kid can look at him and say, "If Dee can do that, I can do it." I think that's a great thing.

I don't think there's any doubt that whatever Dee does in life, he's going to be a success. He proved that to me each and every day. When I think about my time coaching Dee Brown, I'll think about the way he came to play—not just on game days, but at practice, too. He came with energy and enthusiasm and passion for the game. That's what always struck me about him, and what I think will stick with me: Every day that he had the chance, he made the most of it. I'll always remember his passion for basketball, and for life.

Illinois coach Bruce Weber watches Dee shoot free throws during practice at the RCA Dome prior to the Illini's 2005 NCAA tournament first-round game against Farleigh Dickinson.
John Dixon/The News-Gazette

Mark Cowan/Icon SMI

ACKNOWLEDGMENTS

The entire staff of *The News-Gazette* contributed to the coverage of Dee Brown's career and Illinois men's basketball. We gratefully acknowledge the efforts of the sports and photography departments:

SPORTS DEPARTMENT

Sports Editor: Jim Rossow

Illinois men's basketball beat writer: Brett Dawson

Columnist: Loren Tate

Staff writers: Bob Asmussen, Tony Bleill, Brian Dietz, Jeff Huth, Fred Kroner, Jeff Mezydlo

Copy editors: Rich Barak, Mike Goebel, Tony Mancuso, Jason Randall

PHOTOGRAPHY DEPARTMENT

Photo editor: Darrell Hoemann

Photographers: Vanda Bidwell, Heather Coit, Rick Danzl, John Dixon, Holly Hart, Robert K. O'Daniell, Robin Scholz, Dan Williams

Mark Cowan/Icon SMI

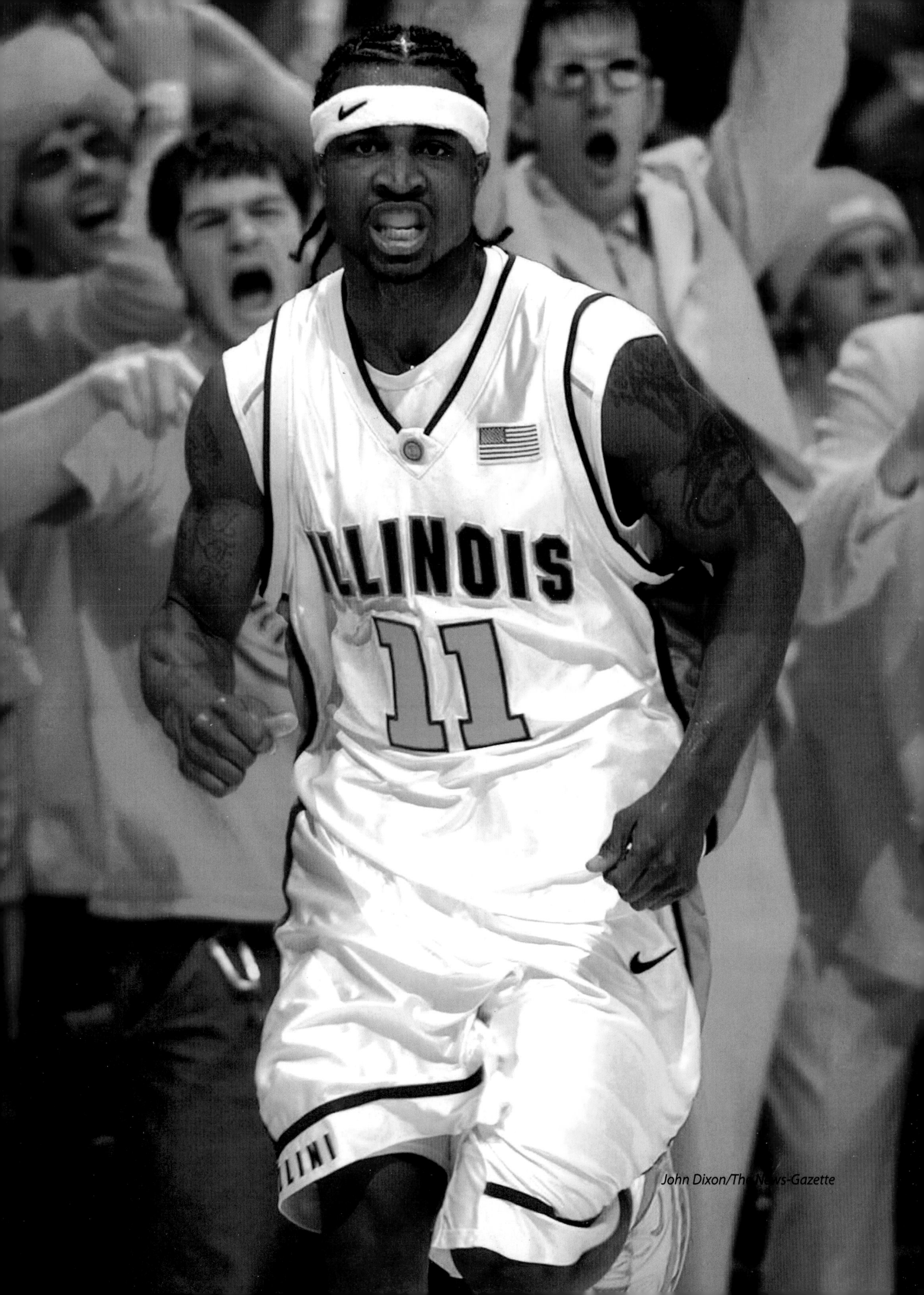

John Dixon/The News-Gazette

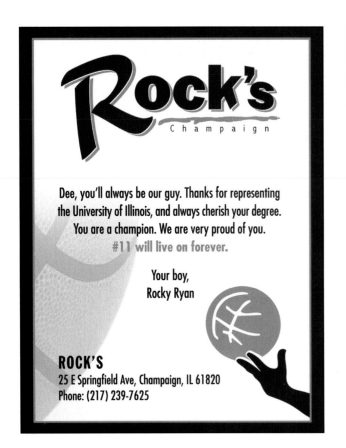

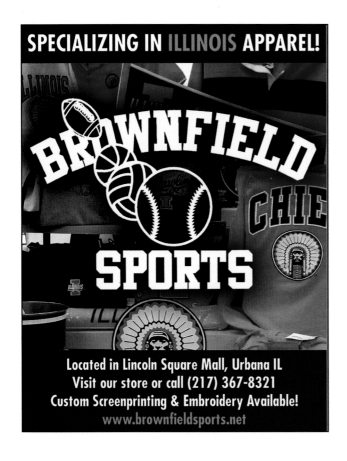